MySQL
Pocket Reference

MySQL
Pocket Reference

George Reese

O'REILLY®

Beijing · Cambridge · Farnham · Köln · Paris · Sebastopol · Taipei · Tokyo

MySQL Pocket Reference
by George Reese

Published by O'Reilly & Associates, Inc., 1005 Gravenstein Highway North, Sebastopol, CA 95472.

O'Reilly & Associates books may be purchased for educational, business, or sales promotional use. Online editions are also available for most titles (*safari.oreilly.com*). For more information, contact our corporate/institutional sales department: (800) 998-9938 or *corporate@oreilly.com*.

Editor:	Andy Oram
Production Editor:	Philip Dangler
Cover Designer:	Ellie Volckhausen
Interior Designer:	David Futato

Printing History:

February 2003: First Edition

0-596-00446-X
[C]   [4/03]

Contents

MySQL Pocket Reference

Introduction

When I fly across the country, I often pass the hours programming on my PowerBook. If that programming involves MySQL, I inevitably end up lugging around the book I co-wrote, *Managing and Using MySQL* (O'Reilly). I don't carry around the book to show it off; the problem is that no matter how experienced you are with MySQL, you never know when you will need to look up the exact syntax of an obscure function or SQL statement.

The *MySQL Pocket Reference* is a quick reference that you can take with you anywhere you go. Instead of racking your brain for the exact syntax of a variant of ALTER TABLE that you generally never use, you can reach into your laptop case and grab this reference. As an experienced MySQL architect, administrator, or programmer, you can look to this reference.

This book does not, however, teach MySQL. I expect that you have learned or are in the process of learning MySQL from a book such as *Managing and Using MySQL*. Though I start with a reference on MySQL installation, it is designed to help you remember the full process of MySQL installation—not to teach you the process.

Acknowledgments

I first would like to thank my editor Andy Oram, as always, for helping me along. I would also like to thank the book's strong technical reviewers, Paul Dubois, Justen Stepka, and Tim Allwine. Finally, I would like to thank my co-authors for *Managing and Using MySQL*, Tim King and Randy Jay Yarger, who helped set the foundation that made this pocket reference possible and necessary.

Conventions

The following conventions are used in this book:

Constant width

> Used to indicate anything that might appear in a program, including keywords, function names, SQL commands, and variable names. This font is also used for code examples, output displayed by commands, and system configuration files.

Constant width bold

> Used to indicate user input.

Constant width italic

> Used to indicate an element (e.g., a filename or variable) that you supply.

Italic

> Used to indicate directory names, filenames, program names, Unix commands, and URLs. This font is also used to introduce new terms and for emphasis.

Installation

You can install MySQL by compiling the source code with the options that best suit your needs, or by downloading and installing a prebuilt binary. In general, you'll want to use the package management system (such as the BSD ports system) appropriate to your operating system. You can also find both binary and source code at the MySQL web site, *http://www.mysql.com*.

Before installing using either approach, you need to prepare your operating system for MySQL. Specifically, you should create a *mysql* user and group under which MySQL will run.

Compilation

Compiling MySQL requires the following steps:

1. Run *configure*

   Configure comes with a host of options you can specify using the syntax configure --*option[=value]*. For example, configure --prefix=/usr/local/mysql tells the installer to use */usr/local/mysql* as its installation directory.

2. Run *make*

   This step performs the actual compilation.

3. Run *make install*

   This step takes the compiled binaries and installs all components of MySQL in their proper locations.

4. Under Unix, make sure directory owners are all in order.

   ```
   chown -R root {INSTALL_DIR}
   chgrp -R mysql {INSTALL_DIR}
   chown -R mysql {DATA_DIR}
   ```

Configuration

MySQL has three different kinds of configuration, both for the server process at server startup and for the client processes when a user executes them. In order of preference, these configuration options include:

1. Command-line options
2. Configuration file options
3. Environment variable options

In other words, if you have the password option specified on the command line, in your configuration file, and in an environment variable, the command-line option wins. Table 1 shows a list of configuration options. Each option applies to one or more MySQL tools, depending on the context.

Table 1. MySQL configuration options

Option	Description
basedir=*directory*	Specifies the root directory of your MySQL install.
batch	Executes in batch mode, meaning no command-line prompts or other information is sent to stdout. This is the default mode when used with a pipe.
character-sets-dir=*directory*	Specifies where your character set files are stored.
compress	Tells the client and server to use compression in the network protocol.
datadir=*directory*	Specifies the location of MySQL's data files.
debug=*filename*	Specifies a file to send debug information to.
force	Indicates that you want processing to continue for client utilities even when an error is encountered.
host=*hostname*	Identifies the host to which a client should connect by default.
language=*language*	Specifies the language to use for localization.
log=*filename*	Specifies the file to which connections and queries should be logged.
log-isam=*filename*	Specifies the file to which isam changes should be logged.
password=*password*	Specifies a default password for clients to use to connect.
port=*port_#*	Specifies the port number to which the server should listen and to which clients should connect.

Table 1. MySQL configuration options (continued)

Option	Description
silent	Silently exit if a connection failure occurs.
skip-new-routines	Tells the MySQL server to avoid new, potential buggy routines.
skip-grant-tables	Tells the server to ignore all grant tables, effectively giving all users full access to the database server.
skip-locking	Potentially provides better system performance by avoiding system locking. It should not be used in conjunction with *isamchk* or *myisamchk*.
sleep=*seconds*	Sleep between commands.
socket=*name*	Socket file to use for local connections.
user=*username*	Specifies the user name to use for client connections.
variable-name =*value*	Sets the specified variable name to a particular value.
verbose	Tells MySQL to talk more about what is happening.
wait	Tells the client to wait after a connection failure and then retry the connection.

A MySQL configuration file has the following format:

```
# Example MySQL configuration file
#
# These options go to all clients
[client]
password        = my_password
port            = 3306
socket          = /var/lib/mysql/mysql.sock

# These options are specifically targeted at the mysqld
server
[mysqld]
port            = 3306
socket          = /var/lib/mysql/mysql.sock
skip-locking
set-variable    = max_allowed_packet=1M
```

MySQL supports multiple configuration files. As a general rule, it checks files in the following order of preference:

1. User configuration file (Unix only).
2. Configuration file specified through the --defaults-extra-file=*filename* option.
3. A configuration file in the MySQL data directory.
4. The system configuration file.

In all cases except the command-line and user configuration options, the name of the configuration file on Unix is *my.cnf* and on Windows is *my.ini*. A Unix user can override system configuration information by building their own configuration file in ~/.*my.cnf*. The system configuration file on a Unix system is */etc/my.cnf*. Windows, on the other hand, has two system configuration locations, in order of preference:

1. *C:\my.cnf*
2. *C:\WINNT\System32\my.cnf*

You can alternately specify a file on the command line using the --defaults-file=*filename* option. This option causes all options specified in other files to be ignored, even if they are not overridden in the file you specify.

Startup

In general, you will want MySQL to begin running when the operating system comes up. How you do this depends on your operating system.

Mac OS X

Mac OS X automatically executes all scripts under the */Library/StartupItems* directory when the system boots up. If that directory does not yet exist, you will need to create it. For MySQL, you should create the directory */Library/StartupItems/MySQL* and place the startup shell script

MySQL and the configuration file *StartupParameters.plist* in that directory.

Once those files are set up, you need to edit the host configuration file */etc/hostconfig* and add the line:

```
MYSQLSERVER=-YES-
```

MySQL. The shell script to start, stop, and restart MySQL looks like this:

```sh
#!/bin/sh

. /etc/rc.common

StartService()
{
    if [ "${MYSQLSERVER:=-NO-}" = "-YES-" ]; then
        ConsoleMessage "Starting MySQL"
        cd /usr/local/mysql
        bin/mysqld_safe --user=mysql &
    fi
}

StopService()
{
    ConsoleMessage "Stopping MySQL"
    /usr/local/mysql/bin/mysqladmin shutdown
}

RestartService()
{
    if [ "${MYSQLSERVER:=-NO-}" = "-YES-" ]; then
        ConsoleMessage "Restarting MySQL"
        StopService
        StartService
    else
        StopService
    fi
}

RunService "$1"
```

StartupParameters.plist. The configuration file looks like this:

```
<?xml version="1.0" encoding="UTF-8"?>
<!DOCTYPE plist SYSTEM "file://localhost/System/Library/
DTDs/PropertyList.dtd">

<plist version="0.9">
  <dict>
    <key>Description</key>
    <string>MySQL Database Server</string>
    <key>Provides</key>
    <array>
      <string>MySQL</string>
    </array>
    <key>Requires</key>
    <array>
      <string>Network</string>
    </array>
    <key>OrderPreference</key>
    <string>Late</string>
  </dict
</plist>
```

Once installed, you should run the *mysql_install_db* tool to set up your databases.

Other Unix

Setting up other variants of Unix is as simple as copying the script *mysql.server* from the source's *support-files* directory to your version of Unix's startup directory and making sure it is executable by root. Under FreeBSD, for example, place this script in */usr/local/etc/rc.d*.

Once installed, you should run the *mysql_install_db* tool to set up your databases.

Windows 2000/XP

To startup an application at system startup on the Windows platform, you need to install it as a Windows service. You can do this by hand using the command:

```
C:\> c:\mysql\bin\mysqld-nt --install
```

A more convenient way to do accomplish this task is through the *winmysqladmin.exe* utility that comes with the Windows installation of MySQL.

Set the Root Password

After starting the server, and before doing anything else, set a password for the root user:

```
mysqladmin -u root password a_good_password
```

Command-Line Tools

You can interact with MySQL entirely from the command line. In general, each MySQL command accepts as an argument any appropriate option from the configuration options listed earlier. You prefix any such option with two dashes:

```
mysql --password=mypass
```

In addition, each of these options has a short form:

```
mysql -p mypass
```

To see which options apply to individual commands and their short forms, refer to the manpage for the command in question:

```
[23:00:03] george@firenze$ man -M/usr/local/mysql/man
mysql
MYSQL(1)
MYSQL(1)

NAME
     mysql  -  text-based client for mysqld, a
              SQL-based relational database daemon

SYNOPSIS
     mysql [-B|--batch] [-#|--debug= logfile]
     [-T|--debug-info] [-e|--exec=  command] [-f|--force]
     [-?|--help] [-h|--host=hostname] [-n|--unbuffered]
     [-p[pwd]] [--password=[pwd]] [-P|--port=  pnum]
     [-q|--quick] [-r|--raw] [-s|--silent]
```

```
        [-S|--socket= snum] [-u|--user= uname]
        [-v|--verbose] [-V|--version] [-w|--wait]
```

DESCRIPTION
    The mysql program provides a curses-based interface to
    the SQL-based database server daemon, mysqld(1). Full
    fuller documentation, refer to the HTML documents
    installed with the package.

OPTIONS
    -B|--batch
        Print results with a tab as separator, each row on

MySQL provides the following command-line tools:

isamchk

This tool verifies the integrity of your databases and potentially fixes any problems with them. It should be used only on ISAM tables.

msql2mysql

This utility is handy for people converting applications written for mSQL to MySQL. These days, however, few people need this help.

myisamchk

This tool does for MyISAM tables what *isamchk* does for ISAM tables.

mysql

The MySQL interactive SQL interpreter. It enables you to execute SQL on the command line. You can span your SQL across any number of lines. The tool executes your SQL when you terminate it with a semi-colon or the escape sequence \g.

mysqladmin

The MySQL administrative interface. Though many of this tool's functions can be accomplished using SQL and the mysql command-line utility, it nevertheless provides a quick way to perform an administrative task straight from the Unix command line without entering an SQL interpreter. You can specifically execute the following administrative commands:

create *databasename*
> Creates the specified database.

drop *databasename*
> The opposite of create, this command destroys the specified database.

extended-status
> Provides an extended status message from the server.

flush-hosts
> Flushes all cached hosts.

flush-logs
> Flushes all logs.

flush-status
> Flushes all status variables.

flush-tables
> Flushes all tables.

flush-threads
> Flushes the thread cache.

flush-privileges
> Forces MySQL to reload all grant tables.

kill *id[,id]*
> Kills the specified MySQL threads.

password *new_password*
> Sets the password for the user to the specified new password. mysqladmin -u root password *new_password* should be the first thing you do with any new MySQL install.

ping
> Verifies that *mysqld* is actually running.

processlist
> Shows the active MySQL threads. You can kill these threads with the mysqladmin `kill` command.

reload
> Reloads the grant tables.

refresh
> Flushes all tables, closes all log files, then opens them again.

shutdown
> Shuts MySQL down.

status
> Shows an abbreviated server status.

variables
> Prints out available variables.

version
> Displays the server version information.

mysqlaccess
> A command-line interface for managing users. This tool is basically a shortcut for the SQL GRANT command.

mysqld
> The MySQL server process. You should never start this directly, instead use *mysqld_safe* (*safe_mysqld* in pre-4.0 versions).

mysqld_safe
> The server process manager. Under MySQL versions prior to MySQL 4.0, this script is called *safe_mysqld*. It is a process that starts up the *mysqld* server process and restarts it should it crash. Note that the *mysql.server* startup script executes *mysqld_safe* as the appropriate user at server startup.

mysqldump
> Dumps the state of a MySQL database or set of databases to a text file. You can later use this text file to restore the databases you dumped.

mysqlimport

Imports text files in a variety of formats into your database. It expects the base name (the name of the file without its extension) to match the name of the table to be used in the import.

mysqlshow

Displays the structure of the specified MySQL database objects. You can look at the structure of databases, tables, and columns.

Data Types

For each data type, the syntax shown uses square brackets ([ ]) to indicate optional parts of the syntax. The following example shows how BIGINT is explained in this chapter:

```
BIGINT[(display_size)]
```

This indicates that you can use BIGINT alone or with a display size value. The italics indicate that you do not enter *display_size* literally, but instead enter your own value. Possible uses of BIGINT include:

```
BIGINT
BIGINT(20)
```

In addition to the BIGINT type, many other MySQL data types support the specification of a display size. Unless otherwise specified, this value must be an integer between 1 and 255.

In the following cases, MySQL silently changes the column type you specify in your table creation to something else:

VARCHAR -> CHAR

When the specified VARCHAR column size is less than four characters, it is converted to CHAR.

CHAR -> VARCHAR

When a table has at least one column of a variable length, all CHAR columns greater than three characters in length are converted to VARCHAR.

TIMESTAMP *display sizes*
>   Display sizes for TIMESTAMP fields must be an even value
>   between 2 and 14. A display size of 0 or greater than 14
>   will convert the field to a display size of 14. An odd-val-
>   ued display size will be converted to the next highest
>   even value.

Numerics

MySQL supports all ANSI SQL2 numeric data types. MySQL numeric types break down into two groups: integer and floating point. Within each group, the types differ by the amount of storage required for them.

Numeric types allow you to specify a display size, which affects the way MySQL displays results. The display size bears no relation to the internal storage provided by each data type. In addition, the floating types allow you to option- ally specify the number of digits that follow the decimal point. In such cases, the digits value should be an integer from 0 to 30 that is at most two less than the display size. If you do make the digits value greater than two less than the display size, the display size will automatically change to two more than the digits value. For instance, MySQL automati- cally changes FLOAT(6,5) to FLOAT(7,5).

When you insert a value into a column that requires more storage than the data type allows, it will be clipped to the minimum (negative values) or maximum (positive values) value for that data type. MySQL will issue a warning when such clipping occurs during ALTER TABLE, LOAD DATA INFILE, UPDATE, and multirow INSERT statements.

The AUTO_INCREMENT attribute may be supplied for at most one column of an integer type in a table. The UNSIGNED attribute may be used with any numeric type. An unsigned column may contain only positive integers or floating-point values. The ZEROFILL attribute indicates that the column should be left padded with zeros when displayed by MySQL. The number of zeros padded is determined by the column's display width.

BIGINT

BIGINT[(*display_size*)] [AUTO_INCREMENT] [UNSIGNED] [ZEROFILL]

Storage   8 bytes

Description

Largest integer type, supporting range of whole numbers from -9,223,372,036,854,775,808 to 9,223,372,036,854,775,807 (0 to 18,446,744,073,709,551,615 unsigned). MySQL performs all arithmetic using signed BIGINT or DOUBLE values, but BIGINT has performing arithmetic on unsigned values. You should therefore avoid performing any arithmetic operations on unsigned BIGINT values greater than 9,223,372,036,854,775,807. If you do, you may end up with imprecise results.

DEC

Synonym for DECIMAL.

DECIMAL

DECIMAL[(*precision*, [*scale*])] [ZEROFILL]

Storage   *precision* + 2 bytes

Description

Stores floating-point numbers where precision is critical, such as for monetary values. DECIMAL types require you to specify the precision and scale. The precision is the number of significant digits in the value. The scale is the number of those digits that come after the decimal point. For example, a BALANCE column declared as DECIMAL(9, 2) would store numbers with nine significant digits, two of which are to the right of the decimal point. The range for this declaration would be -9,999,999.99 to 9,999,999. 99. If you specify a number with more decimal points, it is rounded to fit the proper scale. Values beyond the range of the DECIMAL are clipped to fit within the range.

MySQL actually stores DECIMAL values as strings, not as floating-point numbers. It uses one character for each digit, one character for the decimal points when the scale is greater than 0, and one character for the sign of negative numbers. When the scale is 0, the value contains no fractional part. Prior to MySQL 3.23, the precision actually had to include space for the decimal and sign. This requirement is no longer in place, in accordance with the ANSI specification.

ANSI SQL supports the omission of precision and/or scale where the omission of scale creates a default scale of zero and the omission of precision defaults to an implementation-specific value. In the case of MySQL, the default precision is 10.

DOUBLE

DOUBLE[(*display_size, digits*)] [ZEROFILL]

Storage   8 bytes

Description

A double-precision floating-point number. This type stores large floating-point values. DOUBLE columns store negative values from -1.7976931348623157E+308 to -2.2250738585072014E-308, 0, and positive numbers from 2.2250738585072014E-308 to 1.7976931348623157E+308.

DOUBLE PRECISION

Synonym for DOUBLE.

FLOAT

FLOAT[(*display_size, digits*)] [ZEROFILL]

Storage   4 bytes

Description

A single-precision floating-point number. This type is used to store small floating-point numbers. FLOAT columns can store negative values between -3.402823466E+38 and -1.175494351E-38, 0, and positive values between 1.175494351E-38 and 3.402823466E+38.

INT

INT[(*display_size*)] [AUTO_INCREMENT] [UNSIGNED] [ZEROFILL]

Storage   4 bytes

Description

A basic whole number with a range of -2,147,483,648 to 2,147,483,647 (0 to 4,294,967,295 unsigned).

INTEGER

Synonym for INT.

MEDIUMINT

MEDIUMINT[(*display_size*)]   [AUTO_INCREMENT]   [UNSIGNED] [ZEROFILL]

Storage   3 bytes

Description

A basic whole number with a range of -8,388,608 to 8,388,607 (0 to 16,777,215 unsigned).

NUMERIC

Synonym for DECIMAL.

REAL

Synonym for DOUBLE.

SMALLINT

SMALLINT[(*display_size*)] [AUTO_INCREMENT] [UNSIGNED] [ZEROFILL]

Storage   2 bytes

Description

A basic whole number with a range of -32,768 to 32,767 (0 to 65,535 unsigned).

TINYINT

```
TINYINT[(display_size)] [AUTO_INCREMENT] [UNSIGNED] [ZEROFILL]
```

Storage   1 byte

Description

A basic whole number with a range of -128 to 127 (0 to 255 unsigned).

Strings

String data types store various kinds of text data. There are several types to accommodate data of different sizes. For each size, there is a type that sorts and compares entries in a case-insensitive fashion in accordance with the sorting rules for the default character set. A corresponding binary type performs simple byte-by-byte sorts and comparisons. In other words, binary values are case sensitive. For CHAR and VARCHAR, the binary types are declared using the BINARY attribute. The TEXT types, however, have corresponding BLOB types as their binary counterparts.

BLOB

Binary form of TEXT.

CHAR

```
CHAR(size) [BINARY]
```

Size   Specified by the *size* value in a range of to 255 (1 to 255 prior to MySQL 3.23)

| **Storage** | *size* bytes |

Description

A fixed-length text field. String values with fewer characters than the column's size will be right padded with spaces. The right padding is removed on retrieval of the value from the database.

CHAR(0) fields are useful for backward compatibility with legacy systems that no longer store values in the column.

CHARACTER

Synonym for CHAR.

CHARACTER VARYING

Synonym for VARCHAR.

LONGBLOB

Binary form of LONGTEXT.

LONGTEXT

LONGTEXT

| **Size** | 0 to 4,294,967,295 |
| **Storage** | Length of value + 4 bytes |

Description

Storage for large text values. While the theoretical limit on the size of the text that can be stored in a LONGTEXT column exceeds 4 GB, the practical limit is much less due to limitations of the MySQL communication protocol and the amount of memory available to both the client and server ends of the communication.

MEDIUMBLOB

Binary form of MEDIUMTEXT.

MEDIUMTEXT

MEDIUMTEXT

Size   0 to 16,777,215

Storage   Length of value + 3 bytes

Description

Storage for medium-sized text values.

NCHAR

Synonym of CHAR.

NATIONAL CHAR

Synonym of CHAR.

NATIONAL CHARACTER

Synonym of CHAR.

NATIONAL VARCHAR

Synonym of VARCHAR.

TEXT

TEXT

Size   0 to 65,535

Storage   Length of value + 2 bytes

Description

Storage for most text values.

TINYBLOB

Binary form of TINYTEXT.

TINYTEXT

TINYTEXT

Size   0 to 255

Storage   Length of value + 1 byte

Description

Storage for short text values.

VARCHAR

VARCHAR(size) [BINARY]

Size   Specified by the *size* value in a range of 0 to 255 (1 to 255 prior to MySQL 3.23)

Storage   Length of value + 1 byte

Description

Storage for variable-length text. Trailing spaces are removed from VARCHAR values.

Dates

MySQL date types are extremely flexible tools for storing date information. They are also extremely forgiving in the belief that it is up to the application, not the database, to validate date values. MySQL only checks that months range from 0 to 12 and dates range from 0 to 31. February 31, 2001, is therefore a legal MySQL date. More useful, however, is the fact that February 0, 2001, is a legal date. In other words, you can use 0 to signify dates in which you do not know a particular piece of the date.

Though MySQL is somewhat forgiving on the input format, you should attempt to format all date values in your applications in MySQL's native format to avoid any confusion. MySQL always expects the year to be the left-most element of a date format. If you assign an illegal value in an SQL operation, MySQL inserts a zero for that value.

MySQL automatically converts date and time values to integer values when used in an integer context.

DATE

DATE

Format   YYYY-MM-DD (2001-01-01)

Storage   3 bytes

Description

Stores a date in the range of January 1, 1000 ('1000-01-01') to December 31, 9999 ('9999-12-31') in the Gregorian calendar.

DATETIME

DATETIME

Format   YYYY-MM-DD hh:mm:ss (2001-01-01 01:00:00)

Storage   8 bytes

Description

Stores a specific time in the range of 12:00:00 AM, January 1, 1000 ('1000-01-01 00:00:00') to 11:59:59 P.M., December 31, 9999 ('9999-12-31 23:59:59') in the Gregorian calendar.

TIME

TIME

Format   hh:mm:ss (06:00:00)

| **Storage** | 3 bytes |

Description

Stores a time value in the range of midnight ('00:00:00') to one second before midnight ('23:59:59').

TIMESTAMP

TIMESTAMP[(*display_size*)]

| **Format** | YYYYMMDDhhmmss (20010101060000) |
| **Storage** | 4 bytes |

Description

A simple representation of a point in time down to the second in the range of midnight on January 1, 1970, to one minute before midnight on December 31, 2037. Its primary utility is keeping track of table modifications. When you insert a NULL value into a TIMESTAMP column, the current date and time are inserted instead. When you modify any value in a row with a TIMESTAMP column, the first TIMESTAMP column will be automatically updated with the current date and time.

YEAR

YEAR[(*size*)]

| **Format** | YYYY (2001) |
| **Storage** | 1 byte |

Description

Stores a year of the Gregorian calendar. The size parameter enables you to store dates using 2 digit years or 4 digit years. The range for a YEAR(4) is 1900 to 2155; the range for a YEAR(2) is 1970-2069. The default size is YEAR(4).

Complex Types

MySQL's complex data types ENUM and SET are just special string types. We list them separately because they are conceptually more complex and represent a lead into the SQL3 data types that MySQL may support in the future.

ENUM

ENUM(*value1, value2, ...*)

Storage   1-255 members: 1 byte
                256-65,535 members: 2 bytes

Description

Stores one value of a predefined list of possible strings. When you create an ENUM column, you provide a list of all possible values. Inserts and updates are allowed to set the column to values only from that list. Any attempt to insert a value that is not part of the enumeration will cause an empty string to be stored instead.

You may reference the list of possible values by index where the index of the first possible value is 0. For example:

```
SELECT COLID FROM TBL WHERE COLENUM = 0;
```

Assuming COLID is a primary key column and COLENUM is the column of type ENUM, this SQL will retrieve the primary keys of all rows in which the COLENUM value equals the first value of that list. Similarly, sorting on ENUM columns happens according to index, not string value.

The maximum number of elements allowed for an ENUM column is 65,535.

SET

SET(value1, value2, ...)

Storage   1-8 members: 1 byte
                9-16 members: 2 bytes
                17-24 members: 3 bytes
                25-32 members: 4 bytes
                33-64 members: 8 bytes

Description

A list of values taken from a predefined set of values. A field can contain any number—including none—of the strings specified in the SET statement. A SET is basically an ENUM that allows each field to contain more than one of the specified values. A SET, however, is not stored according to index, but as a complex bit map. Given a SET with the members Orange, Apple, Pear, and Banana, each element is represented by an "on" bit in a byte, as shown Table 2.

Table 2. MySQL's representation of set elements

Member	Decimal value	Bitwise representation
Orange	1	0001
Apple	2	0010
Pear	4	0100
Banana	8	1000

In this example, the values Orange and Pear are stored in the database as 5 (0101).

You can store a maximum of 64 values in a SET column. Though you can assign the same value multiple times in an SQL statement updating a SET column, only a single value will actually be stored.

SQL

MySQL fully supports ANSI SQL 92, entry level. A SQL reference for MySQL is thus largely a general SQL reference. Nevertheless, MySQL contains some proprietary enhancements that can help you at the *mysql* command line. This section thus provides a reference for the SQL query language as it is supported in MySQL.

SQL is a kind of controlled English language consisting of verb phrases. Each of these verb phrases begins with an SQL command followed by other SQL keywords, literals, identifiers, or punctuation.

Case Sensitivity

Case-sensitivity in MySQL depends on a variety of factors, including the token in question and the underlying operating system. Table 3 shows the case-sensitivity of different SQL tokens in MySQL.

Table 3. The case-sensitivity of MySQL.

Token type	Case-sensitivity
Keywords	Case-insensitive.
Identifiers (databases and tables)	Dependent on the case-sensitivity for the underlying OS. On all UNIX systems except Mac OS X using HFS+, database and table names are case-sensitive. On Mac OS X using HFS+ and Windows, they are case-insensitive.
Table aliases	Case-sensitive
Column aliases	Case-insensitive

Literals

Literals come in the following varieties:

String
>   String literals may be enclosed either by single or double quotes. If you wish to be ANSI compatible, you should always use single quotes. Within a string literal, you may represent special characters through escape sequences. An escape sequence is a backslash followed by another character to indicate to MySQL that the second character has a meaning other than its normal meaning. Table 4 shows the MySQL escape sequences. Quotes can also be escaped by doubling them up: 'This is a "quote'". However, you do not need to double up on single quotes when the string is enclosed by double quotes: "This is a 'quote'".

Table 4. MySQL escape sequences

Escape sequence	Value
\0	NUL
\'	Single quote
\"	Double quote
\b	Backspace
\n	Newline
\r	Carriage return
\t	Tab
\z	Ctrl-z (workaround for Windows use of Ctrl-z as EOF)
\\	Backslash
\%	Percent sign (only in contexts where a percent sign would be interpreted as a wildcard)
_	Underscore (only in contexts where an underscore would be interpreted as a wildcard)

Binary

Like string literals, binary literals are enclosed in single or double quotes. You must use escape sequences in binary data to escape NUL (ASCII 0), " (ASCII 34), ' (ASCII 39), and \ (ASCII 92).

Decimal

Numbers appear as a sequence of digits. Negative numbers are preceded by a - sign and a . indicates a decimal point. You may also use scientific notation, as in: -45198. 2164e+10.

Hexadecimal

The way in which a hexadecimal is interpreted is dependent on the context. In a numeric context, the hexadecimal literal is treated is a numeric value. In a non-numeric context, it is treated as a binary value. For example, 0x1 + 1 is 2, but 0x4d7953514c by itself is MySQL.

Null

> The special keyword NULL signifies a null literal in SQL. In the context of import files, the special escape sequence \N signifies a null value.

Identifiers

You can reference any given object on a MySQL server—assuming you have the proper rights—using one of the following conventions:

Absolute naming

> Absolute naming specifies the full path of the object you are referencing. For example, the column BALANCE in the table ACCOUNT in the database BANK would be referenced absolutely as:
>
> ```
> BANK.ACCOUNT.BALANCE
> ```

Relative naming

> Relative naming allows you to specify only part of the object's name, with the rest of the name being assumed based on your current context. For example, if you are currently connected to the BANK database, you can reference the BANK.ACCOUNT.BALANCE column as ACCOUNT.BALANCE. In an SQL query where you have specified that you are selecting from the ACCOUNT table, you may reference the column using only BALANCE. You must provide an extra layer of context whenever relative naming might result in ambiguity. An example of such ambiguity would be a SELECT statement pulling from two tables that both have BALANCE columns.

Aliasing

> Aliasing enables you to reference an object using an alternate name that helps avoid both ambiguity and the need to fully qualify a long name.

In general, MySQL allows you to use any character in an identifier. (Older versions of MySQL limited identifiers to valid alphanumeric characters from the default character set, as well as $ and _.) This rule is limited, however, for databases and tables, because these values must be treated as files on the local filesystem. You can therefore use only characters valid for the underlying filesystem's naming conventions in a database or table name. Specifically, you may not use / or . in a database or table name. You can never use NUL (ASCII 0) or ASCII 255 in an identifier.

When an identifier is also an SQL keyword, you must enclose the identifier in backticks:

```
CREATE TABLE 'select' ( 'table' INT NOT NULL PRIMARY KEY
AUTO_INCREMENT);
```

Since Version 3.23.6, MySQL supports the quoting of identifiers using both backticks and double quotes. For ANSI compatibility, however, you should use double quotes for quoting identifiers. You must, however, be running MySQL in ANSI mode.

Comments

You can introduce comments in your SQL to specify text that should not be interpreted by MySQL. This is particularly useful in batch scripts for creating tables and loading data. MySQL specifically supports three kinds of commenting: C, shell-script, and ANSI SQL commenting.

C commenting treats anything between /* and */ as comments. Using this form of commenting, your comments can span multiple lines. For example:

```
/*
 * Creates a table for storing customer account
information.
 */
DROP TABLE IF EXISTS ACCOUNT;

CREATE TABLE ACCOUNT ( ACCOUNT_ID BIGINT NOT NULL
                       PRIMARY KEY AUTO_INCREMENT,
                       BALANCE DECIMAL(9,2) NOT NULL );
```

Within C comments, MySQL still treats single and double quotes as a start to a string literal. In addition, a semicolon in the comment will cause MySQL to think you are done with the current statement.

Shell-script commenting treats anything from a # character to the end of a line as a comment:

```
CREATE TABLE ACCOUNT ( ACCOUNT_ID BIGINT NOT NULL
                       PRIMARY KEY AUTO_INCREMENT,
                       BALANCE DECIMAL(9,2)
                       NOT NULL ); # Not null ok?
```

MySQL does not really support ANSI SQL commenting, but it comes close. ANSI SQL commenting is distinguished by adding -- to the end of a line. MySQL supports two dashes and a space ('-- ') followed by the comment. The space is the non-ANSI part:

```
DROP TABLE IF EXISTS ACCOUNT; -- Drop the table if it
already exists
```

Commands

This section presents the full syntax of all commands accepted by MySQL.

ALTER TABLE

```
ALTER [IGNORE] TABLE table action_list
```

The ALTER statement covers a wide range of actions that modify the structure of a table. This statement is used to add, change, or remove columns from an existing table as well as to remove indexes. To perform modifications on the table, MySQL creates a copy of the table and changes it, meanwhile queuing all table altering queries. When the change is done, the old table is removed and the new table put in its place. At this point the queued queries are performed.

As a safety precaution, if any of the queued queries create duplicate keys that should be unique, the ALTER statement is rolled back and cancelled. If the IGNORE keyword is present in the statement, duplicate unique keys are ignored and the ALTER statement proceeds as normal. Be warned that using IGNORE on an active table with unique keys invites table corruption.

Possible actions in action_list include:

ADD [COLUMN] *create_clause* [FIRST | AFTER *column*]
ADD [COLUMN] (*create_clause*, *create_clause*,...)

Adds a new column to the table. The *create_clause* is the SQL that would define the column in a normal table creation (see CREATE TABLE for the syntax and valid options). The column will be created as the first column if the FIRST keyword is specified. Alternately, you can use the AFTER keyword to specify which column it should be added after. If neither FIRST nor AFTER is specified, the column is added at the end of the table's column list. You may add multiple columns at once by enclosing multiple create clauses separated with commas, inside parentheses.

ADD [CONSTRAINT *symbol*] FOREIGN KEY *name* (*column*, ...)
  [*reference*]

Currently applies only to the InnoDB table type, which supports foreign keys. This syntax adds a foreign key reference to your table.

ADD FULLTEXT [*name*] (*column*, ...)

Adds a new full text index to the table using the specified columns.

ADD INDEX [*name*] (*column*, ...)

Adds an index to the altered table, indexing the specified columns. If the name is omitted, MySQL will choose one automatically.

ADD PRIMARY KEY (*column*, ...)

Adds a primary key consisting of the specified columns to the table. An error occurs if the table already has a primary key.

ADD UNIQUE[*name*] (*column*, ...)

Adds a unique index to the altered table; similar to the ADD INDEX statement.

ALTER [COLUMN] *column* SET DEFAULT *value*

Assigns a new default value for the specified column. The COLUMN keyword is optional and has no effect.

ALTER [COLUMN] *column* DROP DEFAULT

> Drops the current default value for the specified column. A new default value is assigned to the column based on the CREATE statement used to create the table. The COLUMN keyword is optional and has no effect.

DISABLE KEYS

> Tells MySQL to stop updating indexes for MyISAM tables. This clause applies only to non-unique indexes. Because MySQL is more efficient at rebuilding its keys than it is at building them one at a time, you may want to disable keys while performing bulk inserts into a database. You should avoid this trick, however, if you have read operations going against the table while the inserts are running.

ENABLE KEYS

> Recreates the indexes no longer being updated because of a prior call to DISABLE KEYS.

CHANGE [COLUMN] *column create_clause*
MODIFY [COLUMN] *create_clause [FIRST | AFTER column]*

> Alters the definition of a column. This statement is used to change a column from one type to a different type while affecting the data as little as possible. The create clause is the same syntax as in the CREATE TABLE statement. This includes the name of the column. The MODIFY version is the same as CHANGE if the new column has the same name as the old. The COLUMN keyword is optional and has no effect. MySQL will try its best to perform a reasonable conversion. Under no circumstance will MySQL give up and return an error when using this statement; a conversion of some sort will always be performed. With this in mind, you should make a backup of the data before the conversion and immediately check the new values to see if they are reasonable.

DROP [COLUMN] *column*

> Deletes a column from a table. This statement will remove a column and all its data from a table permanently. There is no way to recover data destroyed in this manner other than from backups. All references to this column in indexes will be removed. Any indexes where this was the sole column will be destroyed as well. (The COLUMN keyword is optional and has no effect.)

DROP PRIMARY KEY

> Drops the primary key from the table. If no primary key is found in the table, the first unique key is deleted.

DROP INDEX *key*

> Removes an index from a table. This statement will completely erase an index from a table. This statement will not delete or alter any of the table data itself, only the index data. Therefore, an index removed in this manner can be recreated using the ALTER TABLE ... ADD INDEX statement.

RENAME [AS] *new_table*
RENAME [TO] *new_table*

> Changes the name of the table. This operation does not affect any of the data or indexes within the table, only the table's name. If this statement is performed alone, without any other ALTER TABLE clauses, MySQL will not create a temporary table as with the other clauses, but simply perform a fast Unix-level rename of the table files.

ORDER BY *column* [ASC | DESC]

> Forces the table to be reordered by sorting on the specified column name. The table will no longer be in this order when new rows are inserted. This option is useful for optimizing tables for common sorting queries. You can specify multiple columns.

table_options

> Enables a redefinition of the tables options such as the table type.

Multiple ALTER statements may be combined into one using commas, as in the following example:

```
ALTER TABLE mytable DROP myoldcolumn, ADD mynewcolumn INT
```

To perform any of the ALTER TABLE actions, you must have SELECT, INSERT, DELETE, UPDATE, CREATE, and DROP privileges for the table in question.

Examples

```
# Add the field 'address2' to the table 'people' and make
# it of type 'VARCHAR' with a maximum length of 100.
ALTER TABLE people ADD COLUMN address2 VARCHAR(100)
```

```
# Add two new indexes to the 'hr' table, one regular index
# for the 'salary' field and one unique index for the 'id'
# field. Also, continue operation if duplicate values are
# found while creating the 'id_idx' index
# (very dangerous!).
ALTER TABLE hr ADD INDEX salary_idx ( salary )
ALTER IGNORE TABLE hr ADD UNIQUE id_idx ( id )
# Change the default value of the 'price' field in the
# 'sprockets' table to $19.95.
ALTER TABLE sprockets ALTER price SET DEFAULT '$19.95'
# Remove the default value of the 'middle_name' field in
# the 'names' table.
ALTER TABLE names ALTER middle_name DROP DEFAULT
# Change the type of the field 'profits' from its previous
# value (which was perhaps INTEGER) to BIGINT. The first
# instance of 'profits' is the column to change, and the
# second is part of the create clause.
ALTER TABLE finances CHANGE COLUMN profits profits BIGINT
# Remove the 'secret_stuff' field from the table
# 'not_private_anymore'
ALTER TABLE not_private_anymore DROP secret_stuff
# Delete the named index 'id_index' as well as the primary
# key from the table 'cars'.
ALTER TABLE cars DROP INDEX id_index, DROP PRIMARY KEY
# Rename the table 'rates_current' to 'rates_1997'
ALTER TABLE rates_current RENAME AS rates_1997
```

ANALYZE TABLE

```
ANALYZE TABLE table1, table2, ..., tablen
```

Acquires a read lock on the table and performs an analysis on it for MyISAM and BDB tables. The analysis examines the key distribution in the table. It returns a result set with the following columns:

Table
:   The name of the table.

Op
:   The value analyze.

Msg_type
:   One of status, error, or warning.

Msg_text
:   The message resulting from the analysis.

CREATE DATABASE

```
CREATE DATABASE [IF NOT EXISTS] dbname
```

Creates a new database with the specified name. You must have the proper privileges to create the database. Running this command is the same as running the *mysqladmin create* utility.

Example

```
CREATE DATABASE Bank;
```

CREATE FUNCTION

```
CREATE [AGGREGATE] FUNCTION name
RETURNS return_type SONAME library
```

The CREATE FUNCTION statement allows MySQL statements to access precompiled executable functions known as user-defined functions (UDFs). These functions can perform practically any operation, since they are designed and implemented by the user. The return value of the function can be STRING, for character data; REAL, for floating point numbers; or INTEGER, for integer numbers. MySQL will translate the return value of the C function to the indicated type. The library file that contains the function must be a standard shared library that MySQL can dynamically link into the server.

Example

```
CREATE FUNCTION multiply RETURNS REAL SONAME mymath.so
```

CREATE INDEX

```
CREATE [UNIQUE|FULLTEXT] INDEX name ON table (column, ...)
```

The CREATE INDEX statement is provided for compatibility with other implementations of SQL. In older versions of SQL, this statement does nothing. As of 3.22, this statement is equivalent to the ALTER TABLE ADD INDEX statement. To perform the CREATE INDEX statement, you must have INDEX privileges for the table in question.

The UNIQUE keyword constrains the table to having only one row in which the index columns have a given value. If the index is multicolumn, individual column values may be repeated; the whole index must be unique.

The FULLTEXT keyword enables keyword searching on the indexed column or columns.

Example

```
CREATE UNIQUE INDEX TransIDX ON Translation ( language,
locale, code );
```

CREATE TABLE

```
CREATE [TEMPORARY] TABLE [IF NOT EXISTS] table
(create_clause, ...) [table_options]
[[IGNORE|REPLACE] select]
```

The CREATE TABLE statement defines the structure of a table within the database. This statement is how all MySQL tables are created. If the TEMPORARY keyword is used, the table exists only as long as the current client connection exists, or until you explicitly drop the table.

The IF NOT EXISTS clause tells MySQL to create the table only if the table does not already exist. If the table does exist, nothing happens. If the table exists and IF NOT EXISTS and TEMPORARY are not specified, an error will occur. If TEMPORARY is specified and the table exists but IF NOT EXISTS is not specified, the existing table will simply be invisible to this client for the duration of the new temporary table's life.

The CREATE clause can either define the structure of a specific column or define a meta-structure for the column. A CREATE clause that defines a column consists of the name of the new table followed by any number of field definitions. The syntax of a field definition is:

```
column type [NOT NULL | NULL] [DEFAULT value]
[AUTO_INCREMENT] [PRIMARY KEY] [reference]
```

The modifiers in this syntax are:

AUTO_INCREMENT
> Indicates that the column should be automatically incremented using the current greatest value for that column. Only whole number columns may be auto-incremented.

DEFAULT *value*

> This attribute assigns a default value to a field. If a row is inserted into the table without a value for this field, this value will be inserted. If a default is not defined, a null value is inserted, unless the field is defined as NOT NULL in which case MySQL picks a value based on the type of the field.

NOT NULL

> This attribute guarantees that every entry in the column will have some non-null value. Attempting to insert a NULL value into a field defined with NOT NULL will generate an error.

NULL

> This attribute specifies that the field is allowed to contain NULL values. This is the default if neither this nor the NOT NULL modifier are specified. Fields that are contained within an index cannot contain the NULL modifier. (The attribute will be ignored, without warning, if it does exist in such a field.)

PRIMARY KEY

> This attribute automatically makes the field the primary key (see later) for the table. Only one primary key may exist for a table. Any field that is a primary key must also contain the NOT NULL modifier.

REFERENCES*table* [(*column*, . . .)] [MATCH FULL | MATCH PARTIAL] [ON DELETE *option*] [ON UPDATE *option*]

> Creates a foreign key reference. Currently applies only to the InnoDB table type.

You may specify meta-structure such as indexes and constraints via the following clauses:

FULLTEXT (column, ...)

> Since MySQL 3.23.23, MySQL has supported full text indexing. The use and results of this search are described in the online MySQL reference manual. To create a full text index, use the FULLTEXT keyword:

```
CREATE TABLE Item ( itemid INT NOT NULL PRIMARY KEY,
        name VARCHAR(25) NOT NULL,
        description TEXT NOT NULL,
        FULLTEXT ( name, description )
);
```

INDEX [*name*] (*column, ...*)

Creates a regular index of all of the named columns (KEY and INDEX, in this context, are synonyms). Optionally the index may be given a name. If no name is provided, a name is assigned based on the first column given and a trailing number, if necessary, for uniqueness. If a key contains more than one column, leftmost subsets of those columns are also included in the index. Consider the following index definition:

    INDEX idx1 (name, rank, serial);

When this index is created, the following groups of columns will be indexed:

- name, rank, serial
- name, rank
- name

KEY [*name*] (*column, ...*)

Synonym for INDEX.

PRIMARY KEY

Creates the primary key of the table. A primary key is a special key that can be defined only once in a table. The primary key is a UNIQUE key with the name PRIMARY. Despite its privileged status, it behaves almost the same as every other unique key, except it does not allow NULL values.

UNIQUE [*name*] (*column, ...*)

Creates a special index where every value contained in the index (and therefore in the fields indexed) must be unique. Attempting to insert a value that already exists into a unique index will generate an error. The following would create a unique index of the nicknames field:

    UNIQUE (nicknames);

When indexing character fields (CHAR, VARCHAR, and their synonyms only), it is possible to index only a prefix of the entire field. For example, the following will create an index of the numeric field id along with the first 20 characters of the character field address:

    INDEX adds (id, address(20));

When performing any searches of the field address, only the first 20 characters will be used for comparison, unless more than one match is found that contains the same first 20 characters, in which case a regular search of the data is performed. Therefore, it can be a big performance bonus to index only the number of characters in a text field that you know will make the value unique. This feature is, however, dependent on the underlying table type.

In addition, MySQL supports the following special "types," and the MySQL team is working on adding functionality to support them:

```
FOREIGN KEY (name (column, [column2, . . . ]))
CHECK
```

As of MySQL 3.23, you can specify table options at the end of a CREATE TABLE statement. These options are:

AUTO_INCREMENT = start
> Specifies the first value to be used for an AUTO_INCREMENT column. Works only with MyISAM tables.

AVG_ROW_LENGTH = length
> An option for tables containing large amounts of variable-length data. The average row length is an optimization hint to help MySQL manage this data.

CHECKSUM = 0 or 1
> When set to 1, this option forces MySQL to maintain a checksum for the table to improve data consistency. This option creates a performance penalty.

COMMENT = comment
> Provides a comment for the table. The comment may not exceed 60 characters.

DELAY_KEY_WRITE = 0 or 1
> For MyISAM tables only. When set, this option delays key table updates until the table is closed.

MAX_ROWS = rowcount
> The maximum number of rows you intend to store in the table.

MIN_ROWS = rowcount
> The minimum number of rows you intend to store in the table.

`PACK_KEYS = 0 or 1`

> For MyISAM and ISAM tables only. This option provides a performance booster for read-heavy tables. Set to 1, this option causes smaller keys to be created and thus slows down writes while speeding up reads.

`PASSWORD = 'password'`

> Available only to MySQL customers with special commercial licenses. This option uses the specified password to encrypt the table's *.frm* file. This option has no effect on the standard version of MySQL.

`ROW_FORMAT = DYNAMIC or STATIC`

> For MyISAM tables only. Defines how the rows should be stored in a table.

`TYPE = rowtype`

> Specifies the table type of the database. If the selected table type is not available, the closest table type available is used. For example, BDB is not available yet for Mac OS X. If you specified TYPE=BDB on a Mac OS X system, MySQL will instead create the table as a MyISAM table (the default table type). Supported table types are described later.

Finally, you can create a table and populate it straight from the results of a SQL query:

```
CREATE TABLE tblname SELECT query
```

You must have `CREATE` privileges on a database to use the `CREATE TABLE` statement.

Examples

```
# Create the new empty database 'employees'
CREATE DATABASE employees;
# Create a simple table
CREATE TABLE emp_data ( id INT, name CHAR(50) );
# Create a complex table
CREATE TABLE IF NOT EXISTS emp_review (
 id INT NOT NULL PRIMARY KEY AUTO_INCREMENT,
 emp_id INT NOT NULL REFERENCES emp_data ( id ),
 review TEXT NOT NULL,
 INDEX ( emp_id ),
 FULLTEXT ( review )
) AUTO_INCREMENT = 1, TYPE=InnoDB;
```

```
# Make the function make_coffee (which returns a string
# value and is stored in the myfuncs.so shared library)
# available to MySQL.
CREATE FUNCTION make_coffee RETURNS string SONAME
"myfuncs.so";
# Create a table using the resultss from another query
CREATE TABLE Stadium
SELECT stadiumName, stadiumLocation
FROM City;
```

DELETE

```
DELETE [LOW_PRIORITY | QUICK]
FROM table [WHERE clause] [ORDER BY column, ...]
[LIMIT n]
DELETE [LOW_PRIORITY | QUICK]
table1[.*], table2[.*], ..., tablen[.*]
FROM tablex, tabley, ..., tablez [WHERE clause]
DELETE [LOW_PRIORITY | QUICK]
FROM table1[.*], table2[.*], ..., tablen[.*]
USING references
[WHERE clause]
```

Deletes rows from a table. When used without a WHERE clause, this
will erase the entire table and recreate it as an empty table. With a
WHERE clause, it will delete the rows that match the condition of
the clause. This statement returns the number of rows deleted.

In versions prior to MySQL 4, omitting the WHERE clause will erase
this entire table. This is done by using an efficient method that is
much faster than deleting each row individually. When using this
method, MySQL returns 0 to the user because it has no way of
knowing how many rows it deleted. In the current design, this
method simply deletes all the files associated with the table except
for the file that contains the actual table definition. Therefore, this
is a handy method of zeroing out tables with unrecoverably
corrupt data files. You will lose the data, but the table structure
will still be in place. If you really wish to get a full count of all
deleted tables, use a WHERE clause with an expression that always
evaluates to true:

```
DELETE FROM TBL WHERE 1 = 1;
```

The LOW_PRIORITY modifier causes MySQL to wait until no clients
are reading from the table before executing the delete. For

MyISAM tables, QUICK causes the table handler to suspend the merging of indexes during the DELETE, to enhance the speed of the DELETE.

The LIMIT clause establishes the maximum number of rows that will be deleted in a single shot.

When deleting from MyISAM tables, MySQL simply deletes references in a linked list to the space formerly occupied by the deleted rows. The space itself is not returned to the operating system. Future inserts will eventually occupy the deleted space. If, however, you need the space immediately, run the OPTIMIZE TABLE statement or use the *myisamchk* utility.

The second two syntaxes are new multi-table DELETE statements that enable the deletion of rows from multiple tables. The first is new as of MySQL 4.0.0, and the second was introduced in MySQL 4.0.2.

In the first multi-table DELETE syntax, the FROM clause does not name the tables from which the DELETEs occur. Instead, the objects of the DELETE command are the tables from which the deletes should occur. The FROM clause in this syntax works like a FROM clause in a SELECT in that it names all of the tables that appear either as objects of the DELETE or in the WHERE clause.

I recommend the second multi-table DELETE syntax because it avoids confusion with the single table DELETE. In other words, it deletes rows from the tables specified in the FROM clause. The USING clause describes all the referenced tables in the FROM and WHERE clauses. The following two DELETEs do the exact same thing. Specifically, they delete all records from the emp_data and emp_review tables for employees in a specific department.

```
DELETE emp_data, emp_review
FROM emp_data, emp_review, dept
WHERE dept.id = emp_data.dept_id
AND emp_data.id = emp_review.emp_id
AND dept.id = 32;
DELETE FROM emp_data, emp_review
USING emp_data, emp_review, dept
WHERE dept.id = emp_data.dept_id
AND emp_data.id = emp_review.emp_id
AND dept.id = 32;
```

You must have DELETE privileges on a database to use the DELETE statement.

Examples

```
# Erase all of the data (but not the table itself) for the
table 'olddata'.
DELETE FROM olddata
# Erase all records in the 'sales' table where the 'syear'
field is '1995'.
DELETE FROM sales WHERE syear=1995
```

DESCRIBE

```
DESCRIBE table [column]
DESC table [column]
```

Gives information about a table or column. While this statement works as advertised, its functionality is available (along with much more) in the SHOW statement. This statement is included solely for compatibility with Oracle SQL. The optional column name can contain SQL wildcards, in which case information will be displayed for all matching columns.

Example

```
# Describe the layout of the table 'messy'
DESCRIBE messy
# Show the information about any columns starting
# with 'my_' in the 'big' table.
# Remember: '_' is a wildcard, too, so it must be
# escaped to be used literally.
DESC big my\_%
```

DESC

Synonym for DESCRIBE.

DROP DATABASE

```
DROP DATABASE [IF EXISTS] name
```

Permanently remove a database from MySQL. Once you execute this statement, none of the tables or data that made up the database are available. All support files for the database are deleted from the filesystem. The number of files deleted will be returned to the user. This statement is equivalent to running the *mysqladmin drop* utility. As with running *mysqladmin*, you must be the administrative user for MySQL (usually root or mysql) to perform this statement. You may use the IF EXISTS clause to prevent any error message that would result from an attempt to drop a nonexistent table.

DROP FUNCTION

DROP FUNCTION name

Will remove a user-defined function from the running MySQL server process. This does not actually delete the library file containing the function. You may add the function again at any time using the CREATE FUNCTION statement. In the current implementation, DROP FUNCTION simply removes the function from the function table within the MySQL database. This table keeps track of all active functions.

DROP INDEX

DROP INDEX idx_name ON tbl_name

Provides compatibility with other SQL implementations. In older versions of MySQL, this statement does nothing. As of 3.22, this statement is equivalent to ALTER TABLE ... DROP INDEX. To perform the DROP INDEX statement, you must have SELECT, INSERT, DELETE, UPDATE, CREATE, and DROP privileges for the table in question.

DROP TABLE

DROP TABLE [IF EXISTS] name [, name2, ...]
[RESTRICT | CASCADE]

Will erase an entire table permanently. In the current implementation, MySQL simply deletes the files associated with the table. As of 3.22, you may specify IF EXISTS to make MySQL not return an error if you attempt to remove a table that does not exist. The RESTRICT and CASCADE keywords do nothing; they exist solely for ANSI compatibility. You must have DELETE privileges on the table to use this statement.

EXPLAIN

EXPLAIN [*table_name* | *sql_statement*]

Used with a table name, this command is an alias for SHOW COLUMNS FROM *table_name*.

Used with an SQL statement, this command displays verbose information about the order and structure of a SELECT statement. This can be used to see where keys are not being used efficiently. This information is returned as a result set with the following columns:

table
> The name of the table referenced by the result set row explaining the query.

type
> The type of join that will be performed.

possible_keys
> Indicates which indexes MySQL could use to build the join. If this column is empty, there are no relevant indexes and you should probably build some to enhance performance.

key
> Indicates which index MySQL decided to use.

key_len
> Provides the length of the key MySQL decided to use for the join.

ref
> Describes which columns or constants were used with the key to build the join.

rows
> Indicates the number of rows MySQL estimates it will need to examine to perform the query.

Extra
> Additional information indicating how MySQL will perform the query.

Example

```
EXPLAIN SELECT customer.name, product.name FROM customer,
product, purchases
WHERE purchases.customer=customer.id AND purchases.
product=product.id
```

FLUSH

```
FLUSH option[, option...]
```

Flushes or resets various internal processes depending on the options given. You must have RELOAD privileges to execute this statement. The option can be any of the following:

DES_KEY_FILE

> Reloads the DES keys from the file originally specified with the --des-key-file option.

HOSTS

> Empties the cache table that stores hostname information for clients. This should be used if a client changes IP addresses, or if there are errors related to connecting to the host.

LOGS

> Closes all the standard log files and reopens them. This can be used if a log file has changed its inode number. If no specific extension has been given to the update log, a new update log will be opened with the extension incremented by one.

PRIVILEGES

> Reloads all the internal MySQL permissions grant tables. This must be run for any changes to the tables to take effect unless those changes occurred through a GRANT/REVOKE statement.

QUERY CACHE

> For better memory use, this command defragments the query cache but it does not delete queries from the cache.

STATUS

> Resets the status variables that keep track of the current state of the server.

TABLE table
TABLES table, table2, ..., tablen

> Flushes only the specified tables.

TABLES [WITH READ LOCK]
> Closes all currently open tables and flushes any cached data to disk. With a read lock, it acquires a read lock that will not be released until UNLOCK TABLES is issued. Read locks are ineffective with InnoDB tables.

GRANT

```
GRANT privilege
[ (column, ...) ] [, privilege [( column, ...) ] ...]
ON {table} TO user [IDENTIFIED BY 'password']
[, user [IDENTIFIED BY 'password'] ...]
[REQUIRE [{SSL | X509 |
CIPHER cipher [AND]
[ISSUER issuer [AND]]
[SUBJECT subject]]]
[WITH [GRANT OPTION | MAX_QUERIES_PER_HOUR limit]]
```

In versions prior to MySQL 3.22.11, the GRANT statement was recognized but did nothing. In current versions, GRANT is functional. This statement enables access rights to a user (or users). Access can be granted per database, table or individual column. The table can be given as a table within the current database; use * to affect all tables within the current database, *.* to affect all tables within all databases or database.* to affect all tables within the given database.

The following privileges are currently supported:

ALL PRIVILEGES/ALL
> Assigns all privileges except FILE, PROCESS, RELOAD, and SHUTDOWN.

ALTER
> To alter the structure of tables.

CREATE
> To create new tables.

DELETE
> To delete rows from tables.

DROP
> To delete entire tables.

FILE

To create and remove entire databases, as well as manage log files.

INDEX

To create and delete indexes from tables.

INSERT

To insert data into tables.

PROCESS

To kill process threads.

REFERENCES

Not implemented (yet).

RELOAD

To refresh various internal tables (see the FLUSH statement).

SELECT

To read data from tables.

SHUTDOWN

To shut down the database server.

UPDATE

To alter rows within tables.

USAGE

No privileges at all.

The user variable is of the form *user@hostname*. Either the user or the hostname can contain SQL wildcards. When wildcards are used, either the whole name must be quoted, or just the parts with the wildcards (e.g., joe@"%.com " and "joe@%.com" are both valid)*. A user without a hostname is considered to be the same as user@"%".

If you have a global GRANT privilege, you may specify an optional INDENTIFIED BY modifier. If the user in the statement does not exist, it will be created with the given password. Otherwise, the existing user will have her password changed.

---

* In fact, the rules governing when you need to use quotes are more complex. As a good rule of thumb, whenever you have non-alphanumeric characters, quote them.

The GRANT privilege is given to a user with the WITH GRANT OPTION modifier. If this is used, the user may grant any privilege she has to another user. You may alternately chose to limit the number of queries made by a particular user ID through the MAX_QUERIES_PER_HOUR option.

Support for secure SSL encryptions, as well as X.509 authentication, has recently been added to MySQL. The REQUIRE clause enables you to require a user to authenticate in one of these manners and identify the credentials to be used. Just specifying REQUIRE SSL tells MySQL that the user can connect to MySQL using only an SSL connection. Similarly, REQUIRE X509 requires the user to authenticate using an X.509 certificate. You can place the following restrictions on the connection:

ISSUER *issuer*
> Demands that the certificate have the issuer specified.

SUBJECT *subject*
> Not only does the user have to have a valid certificate, but it must have a certificate for the specified subject.

CIPHER *cipher*
> Enables MySQL to enforce a minimum encryption strength. The connection must use one of the ciphers specified here.

Examples

```
# Give full access to joe@carthage for the Account table
GRANT ALL ON bankdb.Account TO joe@carthage;
# Give full access to jane@carthage for the
# Account table and create a user ID for her
GRANT ALL ON bankdb.Account TO jane@carthage IDENTIFIED BY
'mypass';
# Give joe the ability
# to SELECT from any table on the webdb database
GRANT SELECT ON webdb.* TO joe;
# Give joe on the local machine access to everything in
webdb but
# require some special security
GRANT ALL on webdb.* TO joe@localhost
IDENTIFIED BY 'mypass'
REQUIRE SUBJECT 'C=US, ST=MN, L=Minneapolis, O=My Cert,
CN=Joe Friday/Email=joe@localhost'
AND ISSUER='C=US, ST=MN, L=Minneapolis, O=Imaginet,
CN=Joe Friday/Email=joe@localhost'
AND CIPHER='RSA-DES-3DES-SHA';
```

INSERT

```
INSERT [DELAYED | LOW_PRIORITY ] [IGNORE]
[INTO] table [ (column, ...) ]
VALUES ( values [, values... ])

INSERT [DELAYED | LOW_PRIORITY] [IGNORE]
[INTO] table [ (column, ...) ]
SELECT ...

INSERT [DELAYED | LOW_PRIORITY] [IGNORE]
[INTO] table
SET column=value, column=value,...
```

Inserts data into a table. The first form of this statement simply inserts the given values into the given columns. Columns in the table that are not given values are set to their default values or NULL. The second form takes the results of a SELECT query and inserts them into the table. The third form is simply an alternate version of the first form that more explicitly shows which columns correspond with which values. If the DELAYED modifier is present in the first form, all incoming SELECT statements will be given priority over the insert, which will wait until the other activity has finished before inserting the data. In a similar way, using the LOW_PRIORITY modifier with any form of INSERT causes the insertion to be postponed until all other operations from other clients have been finished.

Starting with MySQL 3.22.5, it is possible to insert more than one row into a table at a time. This is done by adding additional value lists to the statement separated by commas.

You must have INSERT privileges to use this statement.

Examples

```
# Insert a record into the 'people' table.
INSERT INTO people ( name, rank, serial_number )
VALUES ( 'Bob Smith', 'Captain', 12345 );
# Copy all records from 'data' that are older than a
certain date into
# 'old_data'. This would usually be followed by deleting
the old data from
# 'data'.
INSERT INTO old_data ( id, date, field )
SELECT ( id, date, field)
```

```
FROM data
WHERE date < 87459300;
# Insert 3 new records into the 'people' table.
INSERT INTO people (name, rank, serial_number )
VALUES ( 'Tim O\'Reilly', 'General', 1),
  ('Andy Oram', 'Major', 4342),
  ('Randy Yarger', 'Private', 9943);
```

KILL

```
KILL thread_id
```

Terminates the specified thread. The thread ID numbers can be found using SHOW PROCESSLIST. Killing threads owned by users other than yourself requires PROCESS privilege. In MySQL 4.x, this privilege is now the SUPER privilege.

Example

```
# Terminate thread 3
KILL 3
```

LOAD

```
LOAD DATA [LOW_PRIORITY | CONCURRENT] [LOCAL]
INFILE file [REPLACE|IGNORE]
INTO TABLE table [delimiters] [(columns)]
```

Reads a text file and inserts its data into a database table. This method of inserting data is much quicker than using multiple INSERT statements. Although the statement may be sent from all clients like any other SQL statement, the file referred to in the statement is assumed to be located on the server unless the LOCAL keyword is used. If the filename does not have a fully qualified path, MySQL looks under the directory of the current database for the file.

With no delimiters specified, LOAD DATA INFILE will assume that the file is tab delimited with character fields, special characters escaped with backslashes (\), and lines terminated with newline characters.

In addition to the default behavior, you may specify your own delimiters using the following keywords. Delimiters apply to all tables in the statement.

FIELDS TERMINATED BY 'c'

Specifies the character used to delimit the fields. Standard C language escape codes can be used to designate special characters. This value may contain more than one character. For example, FIELDS TERMINATED BY ',' denotes a comma-delimited file and FIELDS TERMINATED BY '\t' denotes tab delimited. The default value is tab delimited.

FIELDS ENCLOSED BY 'c'

Specifies the character used to enclose character strings. For example, FIELD ENCLOSED BY '"' would mean that a line containing "one, two", "other", "last" would be taken to have three fields:

- one, two
- other
- last

The default behavior is to assume that no quoting is used in the file.

FIELDS ESCAPED BY 'c'

Specifies the character used to indicate that the next character is not special, even though it would usually be a special character. For example, with FIELDS ESCAPED BY '^' a line consisting of First,Second^,Third,Fourth would be parsed as three fields: "First", "Second,Third", and "Fourth". The exceptions to this rule are the null characters. Assuming the FIELDS ESCAPED BY value is a backslash, \0 indicates an ASCII NUL (character number 0) and \N indicates a MySQL NULL value. The default value is the backslash character. Note that MySQL itself considers the backslash character to be special. Therefore, to indicate backslash in that statement, you must backslash the backslash like this: FIELDS ESCAPED BY '\\'.

IGNORE number LINES

Ignores the specified number of lines before it loads.

LINES TERMINATED BY 'c'

Specifies the character that indicates the start of a new record. This value can contain more than one character. For example,

---

with `LINES TERMINATED BY '.'`, a file consisting of a,b,c.d,e,f. g,h,k. would be parsed as three separate records, each containing three fields. The default is the newline character. This means that by default, MySQL assumes each line is a separate record.

By default, if a value read from the file is the same as an existing value in the table for a field that is part of a unique key, an error is given. If the `REPLACE` keyword is added to the statement, the entire row from the table will be replaced with values from the file. Conversely, the `IGNORE` keyword causes MySQL to ignore the new value and keep the old one.

The word `NULL` encountered in the data file is considered to indicate a null value unless the `FIELDS ENCLOSED BY` character encloses it, or if no `FIELDS ENCLOSED BY` clause is specified.

Using the same character for more than one delimiter can confuse MySQL. For example, `FIELDS TERMINATED BY ',' ENCLOSED BY ','` would produce unpredictable behavior.

If a list of columns is provided, the data is inserted into those particular fields in the table. If no columns are provided, the number of fields in the data must match the number of fields in the table, and they must be in the same order as the fields are defined in the table.

You must have `SELECT` and `INSERT` privileges on the table to use this statement.

Example

```
# Load in the data contained in 'mydata.txt' into the
table 'mydata'. Assume
# that the file is tab delimited with no quotes
surrounding the fields.
LOAD DATA INFILE 'mydata.txt' INTO TABLE mydata
# Load in the data contained in 'newdata.txt' Look for two
comma delimited
# fields and insert their values into the fields 'field1'
and 'field2' in
# the 'newtable' table.
LOAD DATA INFILE 'newdata.txt'
INTO TABLE newtable
FIELDS TERMINATED BY ','
( field1, field2 )
```

LOCK

```
LOCK TABLES name
[AS alias] {READ | [READ LOCAL] | [LOW_PRIORITY] WRITE}
[, name2 [AS alias] {READ | [READ LOCAL] | LOW_PRIORITY]
WRITE, ...]
```

Locks a table for the use of a specific thread. This command is generally used to emulate transactions. If a thread creates a READ lock, all other threads may read from the table, but only the controlling thread can write to the table. If a thread creates a WRITE lock, no other thread may read from or write to the table.

Example

```
# Lock tables 'table1' and 'table3' to prevent updates,
and block all access
# to 'table2'. Also create the alias 't3' for 'table3' in
the current thread.
LOCK TABLES table1 READ, table2 WRITE, table3 AS t3 READ
```

OPTIMIZE

```
OPTIMIZE TABLE name
```

Recreates a table, eliminating any wasted space and sorting any unsorted index pages. Also updates any statistics that are not currently up to date. This task is performed by creating the optimized table as a separate, temporary table and using it to replace the current table. This command currently works only for MyISAM and BDB tables. If you want the syntax to work no matter what table type you use, you should run *mysqld* with --*skip-new* or --*safe-mode* on. Under these circumstances, OPTIMIZE TABLE is an alias for ALTER TABLE.

Example

```
OPTIMIZE TABLE mytable
```

REPLACE

```
REPLACE [DELAYED | LOW_PRIORITY]
INTO table [(column, ...)]
VALUES (value, ...)
```

```
REPLACE [DELAYED | LOW_PRIORITY]
INTO table [(column, ...)]
SELECT select_clause

REPLACE [DELAYED | LOW_PRIORITY]
INTO table
SET column=value, column=value, ...
```

Inserts data into a table, replacing any old data that conflicts. This statement is identical to INSERT except that if a value conflicts with an existing unique key, the new value replaces the old one. The first form of this statement simply inserts the given values into the given columns. Columns in the table that are not given values are set to their default values or to NULL. The second form takes the results of a SELECT query and inserts them into the table. The final form inserts specific values using a syntax similar to an UPDATE statement.

Examples

```
# Insert a record into the 'people' table.
REPLACE INTO people ( name, rank, serial_number )
VALUES ( 'Bob Smith', 'Captain', 12345 )
# Copy all records from 'data' that are older than a
certain date into
# 'old_data'. This would usually be followed by deleting
the old data from
# 'data'.
REPLACE INTO old_data ( id, date, field )
SELECT ( id, date, field)
FROM data
WHERE date < 87459300
```

REVOKE

```
REVOKE privilege [(column, ...)] [, privilege [(column, ...) .
..]
ON table FROM user
```

Removes a privilege from a user. The values of privilege, table, and user are the same as for the GRANT statement. You must have the GRANT privilege to be able to execute this statement.

SELECT

```
SELECT [STRAIGHT_JOIN]
[SQL_SMALL_RESULT] [SQL_BIG_RESULT] [SQL_BUFFER_RESULT]
[SQL_CACHE | SQL_NO_CACHE] [SQL_CALC_FOUND_ROWS]
[HIGH_PRIORITY]
[DISTINCT | | DISTINCTROW | ALL]
column [[AS] alias][, ...]
[INTO {OUTFILE | DUMPFILE} 'filename' delimiters]
[FROM table [[AS] alias]
[USE INDEX (keys)] [IGNORE INDEX (keys)][, ...]
[constraints]]
[UNION [ALL] select substatement]
```

Retrieves data from a database. The SELECT statement is the primary method of reading data from database tables.

If the DISTINCT keyword is present, only one row of data will be output for every group of rows that is identical. The ALL keyword is the opposite of DISTINCT and displays all returned data. The default behavior is ALL. DISTINCT and DISTINCTROWS are synonyms.

MySQL provides several extensions to the basic ANSI SQL syntax that help modify how your query runs:

HIGH_PRIORITY

Increases the priority with which the query is run, even to the extent of ignoring tables waiting to be locked for update. You can cause database updates to grind to a halt if you use this option with long-running queries.

STRAIGHT_JOIN

If you specify more than one table, MySQL will automatically join the tables so that you can compare values between them. In cases where MySQL does not perform the join in an efficient manner, you can specify STRAIGHT_JOIN to force MySQL to join the tables in the order you enter them in the query.

SQL_BUFFER_RESULT

Forces MySQL to store the result in a temporary table.

SQL_CALC_FOUND_ROWS

Enables you to find out how many rows the query would return without a LIMIT clause. You can retrieve this value using SELECT FOUND_ROWS( ).

SQL_BIG_RESULT
SQL_SMALL_RESULT

Tells MySQL what size you think the result set will be for use with GROUP BY or DISTINCT. With small results, MySQL will place the results in fast temporary tables instead of using sorting. Big results, however, will be placed in disk-based temporary tables and use sorting.

SQL_CACHE
SQL_NO_CACHE

SQL_NO_CACHE dictates that MySQL should not store the query results in a query cache. SQL_CACHE, on the other hand, indicates that the results should be stored in a query cache if you are using cache on demand (SQL_QUERY_CACHE_TYPE=2).

The selected columns' values can be any one of the following:

Aliases

Any complex column name or function can be simplified by creating an alias for it. The value can be referred to by its alias anywhere else in the SELECT statement (e.g., SELECT DATE_FORMAT(date,"%W, %M %d %Y") as nice_date FROM calendar). You cannot use aliases in WHERE clauses, as their values are not be calculated at that point.

Column names

These can be specified as column, table.column or database.table.column. The longer forms are necessary only to disambiguate columns with the same name, but can be used at any time (e.g., SELECT name FROM people; SELECT mydata.people.name FROM people).

Functions

MySQL supports a wide range of built-in functions such as SELECT COS(angle) FROM triangle (see later). In addition, user defined functions can be added at any time using the CREATE FUNCTION statement.

By default, MySQL sends all output to the client that sent the query. It is possible however, to have the output redirected to a file. In this way you can dump the contents of a table (or selected parts of it) to a formatted file that can either be human readable, or formatted for easy parsing by another database system.

The `INTO OUTFILE 'filename'` modifier is the means in which output redirection is accomplished. With this, the results of the `SELECT` query are put into *filename*. The format of the file is determined by the delimiters arguments, which are the same as the `LOAD DATA INFILE` statement with the following additions:

- The `OPTIONALLY` keyword may be added to the `FIELDS ENCLOSED BY` modifier. This will cause MySQL to treat enclosed data as strings and non-enclosed data as numeric.

- Removing all field delimiters (i.e., `FIELDS TERMINATED BY " ENCLOSED BY "`) will cause a fixed-width format to be used. Data will be exported according to the display size of each field. Many spreadsheets and desktop databases can import fixed-width format files. You must have `FILE` permissions to execute this command.

The default behavior with no delimiters is to export tab delimited data using backslash (\) as the escape character and to write one record per line. You may optionally specify a `DUMPFILE` instead of an `OUTFILE`. This syntax will cause a single row to be placed into the file with no field or line separators. It is used for outputting binary fields.

The list of tables to join may be specified in the following ways:

`Table1, Table2, Table3, . . .`
> This is the simplest form. The tables are joined in the manner that MySQL deems most efficient. This method can also be written as `Table1 JOIN Table2 JOIN Table3, ...`. The `CROSS` keyword can also be used, but it has no effect (e.g., `Table1 CROSS JOIN Table2`) Only rows that match the conditions for both columns are included in the joined table. For example, `SELECT * FROM people, homes WHERE people.id=homes.owner` would create a joined table containing the rows in the `people` table that have `id` fields that match the `owner` field in the `homes` table.

> Like values, table names can also be aliased (e.g., `SELECT t1. name, t2.address FROM long_table_name t1, longer_table_ name t2`)

Table1 INNER JOIN *Table2* {[ON *expr*] | [USING (*columns*)]}

Performs a standard inner join. This method is identical to the method just described, except you specify the USING clause to describe the join columns instead of a WHERE clause.

Table1 STRAIGHT_JOIN *Table2*

This is identical to the first method, except that the left table is always read before the right table. This should be used if MySQL performs inefficient sorts by joining the tables in the wrong order.

Table1 LEFT [OUTER] JOIN *Table2* ON *expression*

This checks the right table against the clause. For each row that does not match, a row of NULLs is used to join with the left table. Using the previous example, SELECT * FROM people, homes LEFT JOIN people, homes ON people.id=homes.owner, the joined table would contain all the rows that match in both tables, as well as any rows in the people table that do not have matching rows in the homes table; NULL values would be used for the homes fields in these rows. The OUTER keyword is optional and has no effect.

Table1 LEFT [OUTER] JOIN *Table2* USING (*column*[, *column2* . . .])

This joins the specified columns only if they exist in both tables (e.g., SELECT * FROM old LEFT OUTER JOIN new USING (id)).

Table1 NATURAL LEFT [OUTER] JOIN *Table2*

This joins only the columns that exist in both tables. This would be the same as using the previous method and specifying all the columns in both tables (e.g., SELECT rich_people. salary, poor_people.salary FROM rich_people NATURAL LEFT JOIN poor_people).

{oj *Table1* LEFT OUTER JOIN *Table2* ON *clause* }

This is identical to *Table1* LEFT JOIN *Table2* ON *clause* and is included only for ODBC compatibility.

MySQL also supports right joins using the same syntax as left joins—except for the OJ syntax. For portability, however, it is recommended that you formulate your joins as left joins.

If no constraints are provided, SELECT returns all the data in the selected tables. You may also optionally tell MySQL whether to use or ignore specific indexes on a join using USE INDEX and IGNORE INDEX.

The search constraints can contain any of the following substatements:

WHERE *statement*

> The WHERE statement construct is the most common way of searching for data in SQL. This statement is usually a comparison of some type but can also include any of the following functions, except for the aggregate functions. Named values, such as column names and aliases, and literal numbers and strings can be used in the statement.

FOR UPDATE

> Creates a write lock on the rows returned by the query. This constraint is useful if you intend to immediately modify the query data and update the database.

LOCK IN SHARE MODE

> Creates a shared mode lock on the read so that the query returns no data that is part of an uncommitted transaction.

GROUP BY *column*[, *column2,...*]

> This gathers all the rows that contain data with some value from a certain column. This allows aggregate functions to be performed on the columns (e.g., SELECT name,MAX(age) FROM people GROUP BY name). The column value may be an unsigned integer representing a column number or a formula, instead of an actual column name.

HAVING *clause*

> This is the same as a WHERE clause except it is performed upon the data that has already been retrieved from the database. The HAVING statement is a good place to perform aggregate functions on relatively small sets of data that have been retrieved from large tables. This way, the function does not have to act upon the whole table, only the data that has already been selected (e.g., SELECT name,MAX(age) FROM people GROUP BY name HAVING MAX(age)>80).

ORDER BY *column* [*ASC*|*DESC*][, *column2* [*ASC*|*DESC*],...]

> Sorts the returned data using the given column(s). If DESC is present, the data is sorted in descending order, otherwise ascending order is used (e.g., SELECT name, age FROM people ORDER BY age DESC). Ascending order can also be explicitly

stated with the ASC keyword. As with GROUP BY, the column value may be an unsigned integer or a formula (though not an aggregate), instead of the column name.

LIMIT [*start*,] *rows*

Returns only the specified number of rows. If the start value is supplied, that many rows are skipped before the data is returned. The first row is number (e.g., SELECT url FROM links LIMIT 5,10 returns URLs numbered 5 through 14).

PROCEDURE *name* ([*arg_list*])

In early versions of MySQL, this does not do anything. It was provided to make importing data from other SQL servers easier. Starting with MySQL 3.22, this substatement lets you specify a procedure that modifies the query result before returning it to the client.

SELECT supports functions. MySQL defines several built-in functions that can operate on the data in the table, returning the computed value(s) to the user. With some functions, the value returned depends on whether the user wants to receive a numerical or string value. This is regarded as the "context" of the function. When selecting values to be displayed to the user, only text context is used, but when selecting data to be inserted into a field, or to be used as the argument of another function, the context depends upon what the receiver is expecting. For instance, selecting data to be inserted into a numerical field will place the function into a numerical context.

MySQL 4.0 introduced support for unions. A UNION clause enables the results from two SELECT statements to be joined as a single result set. The two queries should have columns that match in type and number. Matching in type allows for columns to have types that are convertible.

Examples

```
# Find all names in the 'people' table where the 'state'
$field is 'MI'.
SELECT name FROM people WHERE state='MI'
# Display all of the data in the 'mytable' table.
SELECT * FROM mytable
```

SET

`SET OPTION SQL_OPTION=value`

Defines an option for the current session. Values set by this statement are not in effect anywhere but the current connection, and they disappear at the end of the connection. The following options are currently supported:

`AUTOCOMMIT=0 or 1`
> When set to the default value of 1, each statement sent to the database is automatically committed unless preceded by `BEGIN`. Otherwise, you need to send a `COMMIT` or `ROLLBACK` to end a transaction.

`CHARACTER SET charsetname or DEFAULT`
> Changes the character set used by MySQL. Specifying `DEFAULT` will return to the original character set.

`LAST_INSERT_ID=number`
> Determines the value returned from the `LAST_INSERT_ID( )` function.

`PASSWORD=PASSWORD('password')`
> Sets the password for the current user.

`PASSWORD FOR user = PASSWORD('password')`
> Sets the password for the specified user.

`SQL_AUTO_IS_NULL= 0 or 1`
> When set to the default value of 1, you can find the last inserted row in a table with `WHERE auto_increment_column IS NULL`.

`SQL_BIG_SELECTS=0 or 1`
> Determines the behavior when a large `SELECT` query is encountered. If set to 1, MySQL will abort the query with an error, if the query would probably take too long to compute. MySQL decides that a query will take too long if it will have to examine more rows than the value of the `max_join_size` server variable. The default value of the variable is 0, which allows all queries.

`SQL_BIG_TABLES=0 or 1`
> Determines the behavior of temporary tables (usually generated when dealing with large data sets). If this value is 1,

temporary tables are stored on disk, which is slower than primary memory but can prevent errors on systems with low memory. The default value is 0, which stores temporary tables in RAM.

`SQL_BUFFER_RESULT=0 or 1`

A value of 1 is the same as specifying `SQL_BUFFER_RESULT` for every `SELECT` statement. It forces MySQL to place results into a temporary table.

`SQL_LOG_OFF=0 or 1`

When set to 1, turns off standard logging for the current session. This does not stop logging to the ISAM log or the update log. You must have `PROCESS LIST` (`SUPER` as of MySQL 4.0.2) privileges to use this option. The default is 0, which enables standard logging.

`SQL_LOG_UPDATE=0 or 1`

Enables a client to turn off its update log only if the client has `PROCESS` (`SUPER` as of MySQL 4.0.2) privileges.

`SQL_LOW_PRIORITY_UPDATES=0 or 1`

Tells MySQL to wait until no pending `SELECT` or `LOCK TABLE READ` is occurring on an affected table before executing a write statement.

`SQL_MAX_JOIN_SIZE=value or DEFAULT`

Prohibits MySQL from executing queries that will likely need more than the specified number of row combinations. If you set this value to anything other than the default, it will cause `SQL_BIG_SELECTS` to be reset. Resetting `SQL_BIG_SELECTS` will cause this value to be ignored.

`SQL_QUERY_CACHE_TYPE=value`

Tells MySQL not to cache or retrieve results (0 or `OFF`), to cache everything but `SQL_NO_CACHE` queries (1 or `ON`), or to cache only `SQL_CACHE` queries (2 or `DEMAND`).

`SQL_SAFE_UPDATES=0 or 1`

Prevents accidental executions of `UPDATE` or `DELETE` statements that do not have a `WHERE` clause or `LIMIT` set.

SQL_SELECT_LIMIT=*number*

    The maximum number of records returned by a SELECT query.
A LIMIT modifier in a SELECT statement overrides this value.
The default behavior is to return all records.

SQL_UPDATE_LOG=0 or 1

    When set to 0, turns off update logging for the current
session. This does not affect standard logging or ISAM
logging. You must have PROCESS LIST (SUPER as of MySQL 4.0.
2) privileges to use this option. The default is 1, which
enables update logging.

TIMESTAMP=*value* or DEFAULT

    Determines the time used for the session. This time is logged
to the update log and will be used if data is restored from the
log. Specifying DEFAULT will return to the system time.

Example

```
# Turn off logging for the current connection.
SET OPTION SQL_LOG_OFF=1
```

SHOW

```
SHOW [FULL] COLUMNS FROM table [FROM database] [LIKE clause]
SHOW DATABASES [LIKE clause]
SHOW FIELDS FROM table [FROM database] [LIKE clause]
SHOW GRANTS FOR user
SHOW INDEX FROM table [FROM database]
SHOW KEYS FROM table [FROM database]
SHOW LOGS
SHOW MASTER STATUS
SHOW MASTER LOGS
SHOW [FULL] PROCESSLIST
SHOW SLAVE STATUS
SHOW STATUS [LIKE clause]
SHOW TABLE STATUS [FROM database [LIKE clause]]
SHOW [OPEN] TABLES [FROM database] [LIKE clause]
SHOW VARIABLES [LIKE clause]
```

Displays a lot of different information about the MySQL system.
This statement can be used to examine the status or structure of
almost any part of MySQL.

Examples

```
# Show the available databases
SHOW DATABASES;
# Display information on the indexes on table 'bigdata'
SHOW KEYS FROM bigdata;
# Display information on the indexes on table 'bigdata'
# in the database 'mydata'
SHOW INDEX FROM bigdata FROM mydata;
# Show the tables available from the database 'mydata'
# that begin with the letter 'z'
SHOW TABLES FROM mydata LIKE 'z%';
# Display information about the columns on the table
# 'skates'
SHOW COLUMNS FROM stakes;
# Display information about the columns on the table
# 'people' that end with '_name'
SHOW FIELDS FROM people LIKE '%\_name';
# Show the threads
SHOW PROCESSLIST;
# Show server status information.
SHOW STATUS;
# Display server variables
SHOW VARIABLES;
```

TRUNCATE

TRUNCATE TABLE *table*

Drops and recreates the specified table.

Example

```
# Truncate the emp_data table
TRUNCATE TABLE emp_data;
```

UNLOCK

UNLOCK TABLES

Unlocks all tables that were locked using the LOCK statement during the current connection.

Example

```
# Unlock all tables
UNLOCK TABLES
```

UPDATE

```
UPDATE [LOW_PRIORITY] [IGNORE] table
SET column=value, ...
[WHERE clause]
[LIMIT n]
```

Alters data within a table. You may use the name of a column as a value when setting a new value. For example, UPDATE health SET miles_ran=miles_ran+5 would add five to the current value of the miles_ran column.

The WHERE clause limits updates to matching rows. The LIMIT clause ensures that only n rows change. The statement returns the number of rows changed.

You must have UPDATE privileges to use this statement.

Example

```
# Change the name 'John Deo' to 'John Doe' everywhere in
the people table.
UPDATE people SET name='John Doe' WHERE name='John Deo'
```

USE

```
USE database
```

Selects the default database. The database given in this statement is used as the default database for subsequent queries. Other databases may still be explicitly specified using the database.table. column notation.

Example

```
# Make db1 the default database.
USE db1
```

Operators

MySQL offers three kinds of operators: arithmetic, comparison, and logical.

Rules of Precedence

When your SQL contains complex expressions, the subexpressions are evaluated based on MySQL's rules of precedence. Of course, you may always override MySQL's rules of precedence by enclosing an expression in parentheses.

1. BINARY
2. NOT
3. ^
4. - (unary minus)
5. * / %
6. + -
7. << >>
8. &
9. |
10. < <= > >= = <=> <> IN IS LIKE REGEXP
11. BETWEEN CASE
12. AND
13. OR XOR

Arithmetic Operators

Arithmetic operators perform basic arithmetic on two values.

+   Adds two numerical values

-    Subtracts two numerical values

*   Multiplies two numerical values

/   Divides two numerical values

%   Gives the modulo of two numerical values

| | Performs a bitwise OR on two integer values
| ^ | Performs a bitwise exclusive OR on two integer values.
| & | Performs a bitwise AND on two integer values
| << | Performs a bitwise left shift on an integer value
| >> | Performs a bitwise right shift on an integer value

Comparison Operators

Comparison operators compare values and return 1 if the comparison is true and 0 otherwise. Except for the <=> operator, NULL values cause a comparison operator to evaluate to NULL.

<> or !=
   Match rows if the two values are not equal.

<= Match rows if the left value is less than or equal to the right value.

< Match rows if the left value is less than the right value.

>= Match rows if the left value is greater than or equal to the right value.

> Match rows if the left value is greater than the right value.

value BETWEEN *value1* AND *value2*
   Match rows if *value* is between *value1* and *value2*, or equal to one of them.

value IN (*value1,value2,...*)
   Match rows if *value* is among the values listed.

value NOT IN (*value1, value2,...*)
   Match rows if *value* is not among the values listed.

value1 LIKE *value2*
   Compares *value1* to *value2* and matches the rows if they match. The righthand value can contain the wildcard '%', which matches any number of characters (including 0), and '_', which matches exactly one character. Its most common use is comparing a field value with a literal containing a wildcard (e.g., SELECT name FROM people WHERE name LIKE 'B%').

value1 NOT LIKE *value2*

> Compares *value1* to *value2* and matches the rows if they differ. This is identical to NOT (value1 LIKE value2).

value1 REGEXP/RLIKE *value2*

> Compares *value1* to *value2* using the extended regular expression syntax and matches the rows if the two values match. The righthand value can contain full Unix regular expression wildcards and constructs (e.g., SELECT name FROM people WHERE name RLIKE '^B.*').

value1 NOT REGEXP *value2*

> Compares *value1* to *value2* using the extended regular expression syntax and matches the rows if they differ. This is identical to NOT (value1 REXEXP value2).

Logical Operators

Logical operators check the truth value of one or more expressions. In SQL terms, a logical operator checks whether its operands are 0, nonzero, or NULL. A 0 value means false, nonzero means true, and NULL means no value.

NOT *or* !

> Performs a logical not (returns "1" if the value is 0, NULL if it is NULL, otherwise "0").

OR *or* ||

> Performs a logical or (returns "1" if any of the arguments are nonzero and non-NULL, NULL if any are NULL; otherwise, returns "0").

XOR

> Performs a logical exclusive or (returns "1" if one and only on argument is nonzero and non-NULL, NULL if any are NULL; otherwise. returns "0").

AND *or* &&

> Performs a logical and (returns "0" if any of the arguments are 0, NULL if any are NULL; otherwise, returns "1").

Functions

MySQL provides built-in functions that perform special operations.

Aggregate Functions

Aggregate functions operate on a set of data. These are usually used to perform some action on a complete set of returned rows. For example, SELECT AVG(height) FROM kids would return the average of all the values of the height field in the kids table.

AVG(*expression*)
> Returns the average value of the values in *expression* (e.g., SELECT AVG(score) FROM tests).

BIT_AND(*expression*)
> Returns the bitwise AND aggregate of all the values in *expression* (e.g., SELECT BIT_AND(flags) FROM options). A bit will be set in the result if and only if the bit is set in every input field.

BIT_OR(*expression*)
> Returns the bitwise OR aggregate of all the values in *expression* (e.g., SELECT BIT_OR(flags) FROM options). A bit is set in the result if it is set in at least one of the input fields.

COUNT(*expression*)
> Returns the number of times *expression* was not null. COUNT(*) will return the number of rows with some data in the entire table (e.g., SELECT COUNT(*) FROM folders).

MAX(*expression*)
> Returns the largest value in *expression* (e.g., SELECT MAX (elevation) FROM mountains).

MIN(*expression*)
> Returns the smallest value in *expression* (e.g., SELECT MIN(level) FROM toxic_waste).

STD(*expression*)/STDDEV(*expression*)

> Returns the standard deviation of the values in *expression* (e.g., SELECT STDDEV(points) FROM data).

SUM(*expression*)

> Returns the sum of the values in *expression* (e.g., SELECT SUM(calories) FROM daily_diet).

General Functions

General functions operate on one or more discrete values. We have omitted a few rarely used functions with very specialized applications.

ABS(*number*)

> Returns the absolute value of *number* (e.g., ABS(-10) returns "10").

ACOS(*number*)

> Returns the inverse cosine of *number* in radians (e.g., ACOS(0) returns "1.570796").

ADDDATE(*date*, INTERVAL, *amount*, *type*)

> Synonym for DATE_ADD.

ASCII(*char*)

> Returns the ASCII value of the given character (e.g., ASCII(h) returns "104").

ASIN(*number*)

> Returns the inverse sine of *number* in radians (e.g., ASIN(0) returns "0.000000").

ATAN(*number*)

> Returns the inverse tangent of number in radians (e.g., ATAN(1) returns "0.785398").

ATAN2(*X*, *Y*)

> Returns the inverse tangent of the point (*X*,*Y*) (for example, ATAN2(-3,3) returns "-0.785398").

BENCHMARK(*num, function*)

Runs *function* over and over *num* times and reports the total elapsed clock time. Without any arguments, this function returns "0".

BIN(*decimal*)

Returns the binary value of the given decimal number (e. g., BIN(8) returns "1000"). This is equivalent to the function CONV(decimal,10,2).

BIT_COUNT(*number*)

Returns the number of bits that are set to 1 in the binary representation of the number (e.g., BIT_COUNT(17) returns "2").

BIT_LENGTH(*string*)

Returns the number of bits in *string* (the number of characters times 8, for single-byte characters).

CASE *value* WHEN *choice* THEN *returnvalue* ... ELSE *returnvalue* END

Compares *value* to a series of *choice* values or expressions. The first *choice* to match the *value* ends the function and returns the corresponding *returnvalue*. The ELSE *returnvalue* is returned if no *choice* matches.

CEILING(*number*)

Returns the smallest integer greater than or equal to *number* (e.g., CEILING (5.67) returns "6").

CHAR(*num1*[,*num2*,. . .])

Returns a string made from converting each number to the character corresponding to that ASCII value (e.g., CHAR(122) returns "Z").

CHAR_LENGTH(*string*)

Multi-byte character set safe synonym for LENGTH( ).

CHARACTER_LENGTH(*string*)

Multi-byte character set safe synonym for LENGTH( ).

COALESCE(*expr1, expr2, ...*)

Returns the first non-null expression in the list (e.g., COALESCE(NULL, NULL, 'cheese', 2) returns "cheese").

CONCAT(*string1*[,*string2*,*string3*,. . .])

Returns the string formed by joining together all of the arguments (e.g., CONCAT('Hi',' ','Mom','!') returns "Hi Mom!").

CONCAT_WS(*sep*, *string1*, [*string2*, ...])

Returns all strings as a single string, separated by *sep*.

CONNECTION_ID( )

Returns the ID of the current connection.

CONV(*number, base1, base2*)

Returns the value of *number* converted from *base1* to *base2*. *number* must be an integer value (either as a bare number or as a string). The bases can be any integer from 2 to 36. Thus, CONV(8,10,2) returns "1000", which is the number 8 in decimal converted to binary.

COS(*radians*)

Returns the cosine of the given number, which is in radians (e.g., COS(0) returns "1.000000").

COT(*radians*)

Returns the cotangent of the given number, which must be in radians (e.g., COT(1) returns "0.642093").

CURDATE( )

Returns the current date. A number of the form YYYYMMDD is returned if this is used in a numerical context; otherwise, a string of the form 'YYYY-MM-DD' is returned (e.g., CURDATE( ) could return "1998-08-24").

CURRENT_DATE( )

Synonym for CURDATE( ).

CURRENT_TIME( )

Synonym for CURTIME( ).

CURRENT_TIMESTAMP( )

Synonym for NOW( ).

CURTIME( )

Returns the current time. A number of the form HHMMSS is returned if this is used in a numerical context; otherwise, a string of the form HH:MM:SS is returned (e.g., CURTIME( ) could return "13:02:43").

DATABASE( )

> Returns the name of the current database (e.g., DATABASE( ) could return "mydata").

DATE_ADD(*date*, INTERVAL, *amount*, *type*)

> Returns a date formed by adding the given amount of time to the given date. The type element to add can be one of the following: SECOND, MINUTE, HOUR, DAY, MONTH, YEAR, MINUTE_SECOND (as "minutes:seconds"), HOUR_MINUTE (as "hours:minutes"), DAY_HOUR (as "days hours"), YEAR_MONTH (as "years-months"), HOUR_SECOND (as "hours:minutes:seconds"), DAY_MINUTE (as "days hours:minutes") and DAY_SECOND (as "days hours:minutes:seconds"). Except for those time elements with specified forms, the amount must be an integer value (e.g., DATE_ADD("1998-08-24 13:00:00", INTERVAL 2 MONTH) returns "1998-10-24 13:00:00").

DATE_FORMAT(*date*, *format*)

> Returns the date formatted as specified. The format string prints as given with the following values substituted:

%a   Short weekday name (Sun, Mon, etc.)

%b   Short month name (Jan, Feb, etc.)

%D   Day of the month with ordinal suffix (1st, 2nd, 3rd, etc.)

%d   Day of the month

%H   24-hour hour (always two digits, e.g., 01)

%h/%I 12-hour hour (always two digits, e.g., 09)

%i   Minutes

%j   Day of the year

%k   24-hour hour (one or two digits, e.g., 1)

%l   12-hour hour (one or two digits, e.g., 9)

%M   Name of the month

%m   Number of the month (January is 1)

%p   A.M. or P.M.

%r	12-hour total time (including A.M./P.M.)
%S	Seconds (always two digits, e.g., 04)
%s	Seconds (one or two digits, e.g., 4)
%T	24-hour total time
%U	Week of the year (new weeks begin on Sunday)
%W	Name of the weekday
%w	Number of weekday (0 is Sunday)
%Y	Four-digit year
%y	Two-digit year
%%	A literal % character

DATE_SUB(*date*, INTERVAL*amount* *type*)

Returns a date formed by subtracting the given amount of time from the given date. The same interval types are used as with DATE_ADD (e.g., SUBDATE("1999-05-20 11:04: 23", INTERVAL 2 DAY) returns "1999-05-18 11:04:23").

DAYNAME(*date*)

Returns the name of the day of the week for the given date (e.g., DAYNAME('1998-08-22') returns "Saturday").

DAYOFMONTH(*date*)

Returns the day of the month for the given date (e.g., DAYOFMONTH('1998-08-22') returns "22").

DAYOFWEEK(*date*)

Returns the number of the day of the week (1 is Sunday) for the given date (e.g., DAY_OF_WEEK('1998-08-22') returns "7").

DAYOFYEAR(*date*)

Returns the day of the year for the given date (e.g., DAYOFYEAR('1983-02-15') returns "46").

DECODE(*blob*, *passphrase*)

Decodes encrypted binary data using the specified passphrase. The encrypted binary is expected to be encrypted with the ENCODE( ) function:

```
mysql>
```

```
SELECT DECODE(ENCODE('open sesame', 'please'),
'please');
```

```
+-----------------------------------------------------+
| DECODE(ENCODE('open sesame', 'please'), 'please')   |
+-----------------------------------------------------+
| open sesame                                         |
+-----------------------------------------------------+
1 row in set (0.01 sec)
```

DEGREES(*radians*)

Returns the given argument converted from radians to degrees (e.g., DEGREES(2*PI( )) returns "360.000000").

ELT(*number,string1,string2, . . .*)

Returns *string1* if *number* is 1, *string2* if *number* is 2, etc. A null value is returned if *number* does not correspond with a string (e.g., ELT(3, "once","twice","thrice","fourth") returns "thrice").

ENCODE(*secret, passphrase*)

Creates a binary encoding of the *secret* using the *passphrase*. You may later decode the secret using DECODE( ) and the passphrase.

ENCRYPT(*string*[,*salt*])

Password-encrypts the given string. If a salt is provided, it is used to add extra obfuscating characters to the encrypted string (e.g., ENCRYPT('mypass','3a') could return "3afi4004idgv").

EXP(*power*)

Returns the number e raised to the given power (e.g., EXP(1) returns "2.718282").

EXPORT_SET(*num, on, off,* [*separator,* [*num_bits*]])

Examines a number and maps the on and off bits in that number to the strings specified by the on and off arguments. In other words, the first string in the output indicates the on/off value of the first (low-order) bit of *num*, the second string reflects the second bit, and so on. Examples:

```
mysql>
SELECT EXPORT_SET(5, "y", "n", "", 8);
```

```
+-----------------------------------+
| EXPORT_SET(5, "y", "n", "", 8)    |
+-----------------------------------+
| ynynnnnn                          |
+-----------------------------------+
1 row in set (0.00 sec)

mysql>
SELECT EXPORT_SET(5, "y", "n", ",", 8);

+-----------------------------------+
| EXPORT_SET(5, "y", "n", ",", 8)   |
+-----------------------------------+
| y,n,y,n,n,n,n,n                   |
+-----------------------------------+
1 row in set (0.00 sec)
```

EXTRACT(interval FROM datetime)

Returns the specified part of a DATETIME (e.g., EXTRACT(YEAR FROM '2001-08-10 19:45:32') returns "2001").

FIELD(string,string1,string2, . . .)

Returns the position in the argument list (starting with string1) of the first string that is identical to string. Returns 0 if no other string matches string (e.g., FIELD('abe','george','john','abe','bill') returns "3").

FIND_IN_SET(string,set)

Returns the position of string within set. The set argument is a series of strings separated by commas (e.g., FIND_IN_SET ('abe','george, john, abe, bill') returns "3").

FLOOR(number)

Returns the largest integer less than or equal to number (e.g., FLOOR(5.67) returns 5).

FORMAT(number,decimals)

Neatly formats the given number, using the given number of decimals (e.g., FORMAT(4432.99134,2) returns "4,432.99").

FROM_DAYS(*days*)

Returns the date that is the given number of days (in which day 1 is Jan 1 of year 1) (e.g., FROM_DAYS(728749) returns "1995-04-02").

FROM_UNIXTIME(*seconds*[, *format*])

Returns the date (in GMT) corresponding to the given number of seconds since the epoch (January 1, 1970 GMT). For example, FROM_UNIXTIME(903981584) returns "1998-08-24 18:00:02". If a format string (using the same format as DATE_FORMAT) is given, the returned time is formatted accordingly.

GET_LOCK(*name*,*seconds*)

Creates a named user-defined lock that waits for the given number of seconds until timeout. This lock can be used for client-side application locking between programs that cooperatively use the same lock names. If the lock is successful, "1" is returned. If the lock times out while waiting, "0" is returned. All others errors return NULL values. Only one named lock may be active at a time during a single session. Running GET_LOCK( ) more than once will silently remove any previous locks. For example: GET_LOCK("mylock",10) could return "1" within the following 10 seconds.

GREATEST(*num1*, *num2*[, *num3*, . . .])

Returns the numerically highest of all the arguments (for example, GREATEST(5,6,68,1,-300) returns "68").

HEX(*decimal*)

Returns the hexadecimal value of the given decimal number (e.g., HEX(90) returns "3a"). This is equivalent to the function CONV(decimal,10,16).

HOUR(*time*)

Returns the hour of the given time (e.g., HOUR('15:33:30') returns "15").

IF(*test*, *value1*, *value2*)

If *test* is true, returns *value1*, otherwise returns *value2* (e.g., IF(1>0,"true","false") returns true).

IFNULL(*value, value2*)

Returns *value* if it is not null; otherwise, returns *value2* (e.g., IFNULL(NULL, "bar") returns "bar").

INSERT(*string,position,length,new*)

Returns the string created by replacing the substring of *string* starting at *position* and going *length* characters with the string *new* (e.g., INSERT('help',3,1,' can jum') returns "he can jump").

INSTR(*string,substring*)

Identical to LOCATE except that the arguments are reversed (e.g., INSTR('makebelieve','lie') returns "7").

INTERVAL(*A,B,C,D, . . .*)

Returns "0" if *A* is the smallest value, "1" if *A* is between *B* and C, 2 if *A* is between *C* and *D*, etc. All values except for *A* must be in order (e.g., INTERVAL(5,2,4,6,8) returns "2", because 5 is in the second interval, between 4 and 6).

ISNULL(*expression*)

Returns "1" if the expression evaluates to NULL; otherwise, returns 0 (e.g., ISNULL(3) returns "0").

LAST_INSERT_ID( )

Returns the last value that was automatically generated for an AUTO_INCREMENT field (e.g., LAST_INSERT_ID( ) could return "4").

LCASE(*string*)

Synonym for LOWER( ).

LEAST(*num1, num2*[, *num3,. . .*])

Returns the numerically smallest of all the arguments (for example, LEAST(5,6,68,1,-20) returns "-20").

LEFT(*string,length*)

Returns *length* characters from the left end of *string* (e.g., LEFT("12345",3) returns "123").

LENGTH(*string*)

Returns the number of bytes in *string* (e.g., LENGTH('Hi Mom!') returns "7").

LOAD_FILE(*filename*)

Reads the contents of the specified file as a string. This file must exist on the server and be world readable. Naturally, you must also have FILE privileges.

LOCATE(*substring*,*string*[,*number*])

Returns the character position of the first occurrence of *substring* within *string* (e.g., LOCATE('SQL','MySQL') returns "3"). If *substring* does not exist in *string*, 0 is returned. If a numerical third argument is supplied to LOCATE, the search for *substring* within *string* does not start until the given position within *string*.

LOG(*number*)

Returns the natural logarithm of *number* (e.g., LOG(2) returns "0.693147").

LOG10(*number*)

Returns the common logarithm of *number* (e.g., LOG10(1000) returns "3.000000").

LOWER(*string*)

Returns *string* with all characters turned into lowercase (e.g., LOWER('BoB') returns "bob").

LPAD(*string*,*length*,*padding*)

Returns *string* with padding added to the left end until the new string is *length* characters long (e.g., LPAD('Merry X-Mas',18,'Ho') returns "HoHoHo Merry X-Mas").

LTRIM(*string*)

Returns *string* with all leading whitespace removed (e.g., LTRIM(' Oops') returns "Oops").

MAKE_SET(*bits*, *string1*, *string2*, ...)

Creates a MySQL SET based on the binary representation of a number by mapping the on bits in the number to string values. The first string will appear in the output if the first (low-order) bit of *bits* is set, the second string will appear if the second bit is set, and so on. Example:

```
mysql>
SELECT MAKE_SET(5, "a", "b", "c", "d", "e", "f");
```

```
+------------------------------------------------+
| MAKE_SET(5, "a", "b", "c", "d", "e", "f") |
+------------------------------------------------+
| a,c                                            |
+------------------------------------------------+
1 row in set (0.01 sec)
```

MD5(*string*)

Creates an MD5 checksum for the specified string. The MD5 checksum is always a string of 32 hexadecimal numbers.

MID(*string,position,length*)

Synonym for SUBSTRING( ) with three arguments.

MINUTE(*time*)

Returns the minute of the given time (e.g., MINUTE('15:33:30') returns "33").

MOD(*num1, num2*)

Returns the modulo of *num1* divided by *num2*. This is the same as the % operator (e.g., MOD(11,3) returns "2").

MONTH(*date*)

Returns the number of the month (1 is January) for the given date (e.g., MONTH('1998-08-22') returns "8").

MONTHNAME(*date*)

Returns the name of the month for the given date (e.g., MONTHNAME('1998-08-22') returns "August").

NOW( )

Returns the current date and time. A number of the form YYYYMMDDHHMMSS is returned if this is used in a numerical context; otherwise, a string of the form 'YYYY-MM-DD HH:MM:SS' is returned (e.g., NOW( ) could return "1998-08-24 12:55:32").

NULLIF(*value, value2*)

Return NULL if *value* and *value2* are equal, or else returns *value* (e.g., NULLIF((5+3)18,1) returns NULL).

OCT(*decimal*)

> Returns the octal value of the given decimal number (e.g., OCT(8) returns "10"). This is equivalent to the function CONV(decimal,10,8).

OCTET_LENGTH(*string*)

> Synonym for LENGTH( ).

ORD(*string*)

> Returns a numeric value corresponding to the first character in *string*. Treats a multi-byte string as a number in base 256. Thus, an 'x' in the first byte is worth 256 times as much as an 'x' in the second byte.

PASSWORD(*string*)

> Returns a password-encrypted version of the given string (e.g., PASSWORD('mypass') could return "3afi4004idgv").

PERIOD_ADD(*date,months*)

> Returns the date formed by adding the given number of months to *date* (which must be of the form YYMM or YYYYMM) (e.g., PERIOD_ADD(9808,14) returns "199910").

PERIOD_DIFF(*date1, date2*)

> Returns the number of months between the two dates (which must be of the form YYMM or YYYYMM) (e.g., PERIOD_DIFF(199901,8901) returns "120").

PI( )

> Returns the value of pi: "3.141593".

POSITION(*substring,string*)

> Synonym for LOCATE( ) with two arguments.

POW(*num1, num2*)

> Returns the value of *num1* raised to the *num2* power (e.g., POWER(3,2) returns "9.000000").

POWER(*num1, num2*)

> Synonym for POW( ).

QUARTER(*date*)

> Returns the number of the quarter of the given date (1 is January–March) (e.g., QUARTER('1998-08-22') returns "3").

RADIANS(*degrees*)

Returns the given argument converted from degrees to radians (e.g., RADIANS(-90) returns "-1.570796").

RAND([*seed*])

Returns a random decimal value between 0 and 1. If an argument is specified, it is used as the seed of the random number generator (e.g., RAND(3) could return 0. 435434).

RELEASE_LOCK(*name*)

Removes the named lock created with the GET_LOCK function. Returns "1" if the release is successful, "0" if it failed because the current thread did not own the lock, and a null value if the lock did not exist. For example, RELEASE_LOCK("mylock").

REPEAT(*string,number*)

Returns a string consisting of the original *string* repeated *number* times. Returns an empty string if *number* is less than or equal to zero (e.g., REPEAT('ma',4) returns "mamamama").

REPLACE(*string,old,new*)

Returns a string that has all occurrences of the substring *old* replaced with *new* (e.g., REPLACE('black jack','ack','oke') returns "bloke joke").

REVERSE(*string*)

Returns the character reverse of *string* (e.g., REVERSE('my bologna') returns "angolob ym").

RIGHT(*string,length*)

Synonym for SUBSTRING( ) with FROM argument (e.g., RIGHT("string",1) returns "g").

ROUND(*number*[,*decimal*])

Returns *number* rounded to the given number of decimals. If no *decimal* argument is supplied, *number* is rounded to an integer (e.g., ROUND(5.67,1) returns "5.7").

RPAD(*string*, *length*, *padding*)

> Returns *string* with *padding* added to the right end until the new string is *length* characters long (e.g., RPAD('Yo',5,'!') returns "Yo!!!").

RTRIM(*string*)

> Returns *string* with all trailing whitespace removed (e.g., RTRIM('Oops ') returns "Oops").

SECOND(*time*)

> Returns the seconds of the given time (e.g., SECOND('15:33:30') returns "30").

SEC_TO_TIME(*seconds*)

> Returns the number of hours, minutes, and seconds in the given number of seconds. A number of the form HHMMSS is returned if this is used in a numerical context; otherwise, a string of the form HH:MM:SS is returned (e.g., SEC_TO_TIME(3666) returns "01:01:06").

SESSION_USER( )

> Synonym for USER( ).

SIGN(*number*)

> Returns -1 if *number* is negative, 0 if it's zero, or 1 if it's positive (e.g., SIGN(4) returns "1").

SIN(*radians*)

> Returns the sine of the given number, which is in radians (e.g., SIN(2*PI( )) returns "0.000000").

SOUNDEX(*string*)

> Returns the Soundex code associated with string (e.g., SOUNDEX('Jello') returns "J400").

SPACE(*number*)

> Returns a string that contains *number* spaces (e.g., SPACE(5) returns "   ").

SQRT(*number*)

> Returns the square root of *number* (e.g., SQRT(16) returns "4.000000").

STRCMP(*string1, string2*)

Returns 0 if the strings are the same, -1 if *string1* would sort before *string2*, or 1 if *string1* would sort after *string2* (e.g., STRCMP('bob','bobbie') returns "-1").

SUBDATE(*date*, INTERVAL*amounttype*)

Synonym for DATE_SUB( ).

SUBSTRING(*string,position*)
SUBSTRING(*string* FROM *position*)

Returns the remaining substring from *string* starting at *position*.

SUBSTRING(*string,position,length*)
SUBSTRING(*string* FROM *position* FOR *length*)

Returns a substring of *string* starting at *position* for *length* characters (e.g., SUBSTRING("123456",3) returns "3456").

SUBSTRING_INDEX(*string,char,number*)

Returns the substring formed by counting *number* of *char* within *string* and then returns everything to the left if the count is positive, or everything to the right if the count is negative (e.g., SUBSTRING_INDEX('1,2,3,4,5',',',3) returns "1,2,3").

SYSDATE( )

Synonym for NOW( ).

SYSTEM_USER( )

Synonym for USER( ).

TAN(*radians*)

Returns the tangent of the given number, which must be in radians (e.g., TAN(0) returns "0.000000").

TIME_FORMAT(*time, format*)

Returns the given time using a format string. The format string is of the same type as DATE_FORMAT, as shown earlier.

TIME_TO_SEC(*time*)

Returns the number of seconds in the *time* argument (e.g., TIME_TO_SEC('01:01:06') returns "3666").

TO_DAYS(*date*)

> Returns the number of days (in which day 1 is Jan 1 of year 1) to the given date. The date may be a value of type DATE, DATETIME, or TIMESTAMP, or a number of the form YYMMDD or YYYYMMDD (e.g., TO_DAYS(19950402) returns "728749").

TRIM([BOTH|LEADING|TRAILING] [*remove*] [FROM] *string*)

> With no modifiers, returns *string* with all trailing and leading whitespace removed. You can specify to remove the leading or trailing whitespace, or both. You can also specify a character other than space to be removed (e.g., TRIM(both '-' from '---look here---') returns "look here").

TRUNCATE*(number, decimals)*

> Returns *number* truncated to the given number of decimals (for example, TRUNCATE(3.33333333,2) returns "3.33").

UCASE(*string*)

> Synonym for UPPER( ).

UNIX_TIMESTAMP([*date*])

> Returns the number of seconds from the epoch (January 1, 1970 GMT) to the given date (in GMT). If no date is given, the number of seconds to the current date is used (e.g., UNIX_TIMESTAMP('1998-08-24   18:00:02') returns "903981584".

UPPER(*string*)

> Returns *string* with all characters turned into uppercase (e.g., UPPER ('Scooby') returns "SCOOBY").

USER( )

> Returns the name of the current user (e.g., SYSTEM_USER( ) could return "ryarger@localhost").

VERSION( )

> Returns the version of the MySQL server itself (e.g., VERSION( ) could return "4.0.2-alpha").

WEEK(*date*)

Returns the week of the year for the given date (e.g., WEEK('1998-12-29') returns "52").

WEEKDAY(*date*)

Returns the numeric value of the day of the week for the specified date. Day numbers start with Monday as 0 and end with Sunday as 6.

YEAR(*date*)

Returns the year of the given date (e.g., YEAR('1998-12-29') returns "1998").

Table Types

Table 5 lists some of the table types supported in most MySQL installations. For truly atomic database transactions, you should use InnoDB tables.

Table 5. MySQL table types

Type	Transactional	Description
BDB	Yes	Transaction-safe tables with page locking
Berkeley_db	Yes	Alias for BDB
HEAP	No	Memory-based table; not persistent
ISAM	No	Obsolete format; replaced by MyISAM
InnoDB	Yes	Transaction-safe tables with row locking
MERGE	No	A collection of MyISAM tables merged as a single table
MyISAM	No	A newer, portable table type to replace ISAM